POWER TEACHING

By Benjamin Mahle

FEARON TEACHER AIDS
Simon & Schuster Supplementary Education Group

Cover illustration by Rose Sheifer

Copyright © 1989 by Fearon Teacher Aids. No part of
this book may be reproduced by any means, transmitted,
or translated into a machine language without written
permission from the publisher

ISBN 0–8224–5192–1

Library of Congress Catalog Card Number 89–84134

Printed in the United States of America
1. 9 8 7 6 5 4 3

CONTENTS

INTRODUCTION

The strategies detailed in this book were taught to me by 2,000 former students and by many colleagues. I want to acknowledge these persons now, before moving on, because most of this book does not applaud them. Most of the examples I use to show how legitimate power is acquired feature students who have erred, and educators (including myself) who have erred in dealing with them. Though I feel this book can lengthen its readers' teaching careers, and increase the enjoyment of those years, it is, necessarily, a short book that draws on only a fraction of the experiences I've had in teaching. In future years when I write of the compassion and professionalism of my colleagues and praise the zest, the humor, and great joys brought to me by students—that book will require many hours to read. Because I love teaching, I wish that were the book I'm writing here.

For years I talked smart at lunch, had big ideas on how to stay sane teaching junior high kids. At first I suggested, "Just roll with the punches" and "Try to see the humor in it." Later I learned those notions were not enough. I became more militant in suggesting that my colleagues be more assertive, more willing to identify what they feel is right and reasonable, and then stand up for their beliefs. Marlene seemed to abide my comments especially well, and when I threatened to write everything down, she encouraged me:

—You write it, and I'll read it.
—Okay, I will.

—What'll you call it?
—*Power Teaching.*
—"Power," eh?
—Today this little boy, a new kid, told me right off that if I hit him, he'd sue me. I told him that we don't hit at this school, but once in a while we give hugs.

Though probably no stranger to hitting, this child less needed assurance that his rights would be respected than he needed to see how his boldness would be tolerated. Marlene not only refused to flutter at his threat, but she measured it exactly: it was a youngster's need to feel powerful in an unknown, possibly hostile setting. In fact, the importance of the exchange was in showing that each person was determined to let the other know that neither would accept powerlessness in their relationship. Marlene readily eschewed hitting, but she gave notice that she might still assert herself physically "once in a while." The boy asserted that he would not be controlled by hitting, but he didn't argue against possibly accepting a hug.

Because the dialogue ended there, both apparently agreed that what had been communicated was reasonable and right: hitting was not okay; hugging may be; and having an opinion and being allowed to express it certainly is.

In *Power Teaching*, I suggest that 99 percent of the time students and teachers share a common understanding of what is "reasonable" and "right." This shared knowledge, taught to me over 15 seasons of teaching junior high kids, has empowered me to teach almost completely free of classroom stress these past few years.

All of us want to improve education. To that end, teachers enroll in weekend workshops, summer classes, read books. Well-meaning administrators contract for presentations by specialists like Tony Gregorc, Madeleine Hunter, Ray McGee, each of whom has had special students who showed them the truth—who inspired and so moved them that now they share that truth neatly packaged, at a fair price. I'm not belittling these offerings—they're good.

But I understand our resistance to accepting them: time crunches, brief lunches, planning, meetings—we're overwhelmed. New strategies require study and practice, and we often do not have either time or energy to invest.

Often I've discounted good information, especially when it's been delivered at a pre-school workshop or during my planning period or, God forbid, after school. It seems most presentations are scheduled at times when we are least likely to welcome them.

Still, some of these offerings have been so galvanizing that I've left feeling guilty at not having saved more disgruntled kids (their faces appear vividly before me now), using the techniques expostulated so confidently and detailed further in the myriad handouts I've carried home.

But in my gut, another feeling competed with my guilt—a sense that something else needed to happen before these fine notions could work for me. Because I hadn't had time to explore and define these yearnings clearly, I allowed them to gnaw and thus add to my frustration, anger, and fear.

Often I was tired or felt defeated, and the last thing my ego needed was a "how-to-fix-your-teaching" by someone who had long ago escaped the daily sweat of the regular classroom.

Perhaps you too are fearful and angry and skeptical—and also a bit envious of those folks whose apparent successes only increase your guilt. After all, if you're like me, you've probably not "humanized," "impacted," and "problem-solved cooperatively" with every kid, using "instructional strategies appropriate to each individual's learning style."

Perhaps you haven't tried new methods, or perhaps you've tried without success. Gradually you've felt less able to roll with the punches—those blows inherent in teaching that marvelous, volatile breed of children we call adolescents. And your sense of humor is shot, dulled by more and more responsibilities relative to dealing not only with your students' learning but with their family lives and socialization as well.

Teaching to the "whole child" has meant accepting responsibilities society used to place with parents, courts, and other institutions. Now we are expected, more than anyone else in their lives, to sleuth out our students' individual needs. Has he a learning disability? Is she being abused? Did he get a good breakfast? Can she hear? Is he or she abusing chemicals? Meanwhile, class sizes increase. No wonder we sometimes feel overwhelmed, angry, powerless.

When I've spoken with colleagues about the face and future of education, my suggested hopes for change are sometimes met with, "Yeah, but it all takes money. . . . Parents don't care like they used to. . . . They (the public, the administration) keep asking us to do more, but they aren't willing to spend more. . . ."

These comments testify to the sense of powerlessness that teachers feel. And certainly if teachers feel powerless to change education, it will never happen. Why this cynicism about the future? about improving education? about trying new things? Perhaps it's because many teachers don't know where to find the power to change—to make their teaching more energetic, more effective, more stress-free.

Power Teaching shows how establishing a legitimate power base in your teaching—a base built on what you know is *reasonable* and *right*—will free you of depressing and energy-draining classroom management problems. Only then will you be willing and able to incorporate the good information of others into your teaching style.

Nothing depresses human beings like powerlessness. There is no more awful feeling: even infants cry out against it. As professional adults, we can attack this adversary with learning.

Power Teaching will also impact lives outside of schools. I know how powerlessness in the workplace translates to negative power being deployed at home. "I go home and kick the dog" is no joke. Each of us has spilled the venom of a bad day onto significant others outside our workplace. That need no longer be, for many strategies drawn here are useful in dealing humanely with our own families and friends—anyone, in fact, who would intentionally (or innocently) attack our bases of personal power. Be open to seeing those possibilities, for transference and creativity are powerful resources too.

Imagine having positive energy to invest in family, hobbies, friends. Imagine sleeping well at night and looking forward to work the next day. Imagine, then explore here. Read at random; sample the offerings. Perhaps you'll find fuel for nourishing hope, for sustaining your spirit, and for nurturing bountiful change.

‖ ■

PART I

The Beginnings of Your Power Base

NIGHTMARE

I still have it occasionally, but during my early years in teaching, the nightmare came nearly every Sunday night. In it, the kids are crazy. My classroom is chaotic. Everyone is talking, shouting. Paper airplanes, like spears, swish about the room, endangering the meek and mighty alike. I am unheard amidst the din, or worse, I'm ignored.

> —People. People. Settle down now; we must get
> started. . . . We have to get on, people. We have a
> lot to cover.
> —Who gives a shit?
> —People. That's enough.
> —Up yours!

Those few who aren't oblivious to me are openly insulting. I select the most belligerent and accost him, eyes ablaze. He doesn't flinch. I grab him by the shoulders and shake him, demanding he shut up. But his head bobs like a balloon, like one of those huge Macy's Parade floats, and it smiles maniacally back at me. I slam it against the chalkboard and it bounces back, still smiling, still yakking. Other balloon-faced kids watch, amused. They point and laugh at my frustration. I smack the face, but it bounces back like a boxer's light punching bag, still wearing a jack-o'-lantern grin.

Now all the kids are balloon heads with Halloween grins, and they dart about the room like apes in a trampoline gymnasium. They hoot and whistle, and swear, and engage in unchecked sexual posturing. They shout and laugh, scribble obscene words and graphics on the chalkboards, and slap each other with erasers. I choke on the cloud of white dust. My eyes water and my nose runs; in just moments my handkerchief is soaked. I flail my arms in front of my face, trying to clear the air and chase the calling and cackling back into their mouths.

They've opened the windows, are throwing books out, and dare each other to crawl out along the ledge, which is four floors up. Several accept the dare. I can't stop them. And there are not enough sharp points in the universe to deflate all those tough vinyl cheering and jeering balloon heads. Not enough darts or knives or . . .

But I find a sharpened pencil and stab at a face. A gash opens across its cheek, blood pours out all over me; I mop hopelessly at the gushing wound with the hanky. The face is still there, grinning insolently beneath wild, wide eyes, laughter bellowing from the salivating mouth, and still others press toward me, daring me to repeat my attack. . . .

I wake in a sweat, knowing I wanted to kill those kids—appalled that I wanted to hurt them, but knowing I had to get control.

Imagine the worst actors you've ever known collected in a single classroom. I've seen classrooms degenerate to almost that, with "good" kids spurred by others toward off-the-wall antics. I've seen my own classrooms too much that way. I've experienced the powerlessness and futility that has driven some colleagues over the edge and away from teaching or to long-term mental rehabilitation. This nightmare is real for some. For me it's a reminder that the difference between chaos and what seems to be chaos is the power base the teacher has established. Since I've learned more about power, I've had far fewer nightmares both in and out of school.

Many teachers and kids are suffering. Angry youngsters often unload their pain in hallways and classrooms, swearing at others, threatening, hurling hate-filled epithets. Their nightmares feature balloon-faced parents, siblings, peers, and teachers, perhaps.

In a classroom supervised by a young sub, students sit with their backs to him as he takes roll. Soon many normally well-behaved kids are changing seats, answering for absent students, and mocking the young man's attempts to gain order.

A co-ed phys-ed class of 44 kids features a boy who has been referred seven times to the principal's office for fighting. At home he extorts money from his mother by threatening to shell her with hockey pucks. Her face wears bruises. A lone teacher, responsible for supervising this boy and 43 other students, is also charged with teaching them swimming, gymnastics, volleyball.

Sadly, these are real nightmares, often involving experienced teachers. These teachers are truly concerned for kids but have not established a base of power from which to issue that concern. They may know their subject areas well. They may sympathize with and especially want to help troubled kids. But they are failing miserably, for kids universally respect power and just as completely despise powerlessness.

Kids know that anyone can offer care but only persons with knowledge and power can deliver it. It is unfortunate—but not surprising—when students view a teacher's initial patience and concern for them as manifestations of weakness. So, teachers who wish to make caring for kids a priority must first earn their respect by demonstrating self-care. Kids must see that you will insist on dignified treatment for yourself, and for your classroom and its property. When they see you have caretaking skills, your credibility with them will discourage manipulation, chaos, and ultimately, the real-life nightmares that daily haunt teachers who extend their concern for others ahead of a genuine and visible concern for themselves. Moreover, they may then consider allowing you to reach them on some emotional level.

NOTHING HERE WILL MEAN ANYTHING IF . . .

Be assured now that if you don't like kids—and of course you can't like teaching—then nothing here will mean anything. If you don't like kids, they know it, and you're simply miscast professionally and need to leave teaching. Nothing here will mean anything then, for *Power Teaching* is based on what is right and what is reasonable. It is wrong and unreasonable for you to teach if you don't like kids.

If, however, you are merely discouraged or looking for answers, something here may mean something. If you are capable of examining your present teaching style, you will find suggestions here that may help you.

For openers, try answering this question: Do you esteem kids regardless of their appearances, racial or social backgrounds, ability levels, interest in school, academic and behavioral histories, your past experiences with their siblings or parents, the opinions of your colleagues, *and* the kinds of music they like? In short, do you avoid bringing biases to your teaching that kids can sense are unreasonable, that could prevent you from starting fresh with them?

Teachers who have these biases are largely humorless. That's too bad. There is so much to enjoy about kids that seems contrary to what we would want for ourselves.

If you have a problem with the disparity between your tastes and those of the kids, think about how much you admire high-wire acts: you'd never attempt such things yourself, but you can appreciate the courage, skill, and individual decisions invested in creating something others can admire. As each of us has a unique teaching style, so every kid has a unique act. We must accept that the costuming, the posturing, is part of that act, and moreover, that these things are likely to be the most important elements of their adolescent lives.

If we scoff at or tread on these things, we invite defiance from students. If we invite students to defy us, we are wrong and unreasonable, and all that I say here about being reasonable and right will mean nothing. Prejudging kids is prejudice. Prejudice is a meanness responsible for most of the problems folks have with one another on this planet; even the simplest life forms react negatively to meanness.

Meanness—prejudice—robs us of any claim to legitimate power. If you are mean and not amenable to change, if you are humorless and not amenable to being cheered—nothing here will mean anything.

Know Your Subjects

Daryl penciled his suicide threat on the blond desk top; I noticed it when I quickly checked the desks after his class had left. I always try to check desks for writing then. Reading desktops keeps me current on who hates whom, who's newly in love, who and what is "gross," and, of course, I sometimes learn who is contemplating suicide.

Most desk writing is absent-minded doodling—testimony to the dash and splashy fabric of my teaching—and when I discover it, I can have the writer clean desks for me the next day. Students are more conscientious after that and doodle instead on their folders or book covers. Anyhow, kids know I read desks, so Daryl got the attention he wanted and the counseling he needed that day.

When students tell me I know what's going on, that's cool but it's less a compliment for me than it is an indictment of the naivete of other staff. I hope I'm not a rarity, for it seems to me teachers are remiss if they don't study their subjects. It's not so hard to learn about kids: notice what they read, what they wear, what they scrawl on folders and book covers and desks. Eavesdrop now and then. Why, it's even okay to talk with them as we do adults. This is especially important at the beginning of a new term.

The Personal Profile Sheet (PPS) that kids complete for me at the end of the first day is a powerful diagnostic tool (a sample is on page 20). In addition to asking the student's name and parents' names (they are not always the same, of course, and knowing this can prevent embarrassment), I also get a home phone number. Having the phone number means I don't have to bother office personnel and it gives me faster access to a parent.

My PPS also asks each child to list favorite and least favorite subjects, best skills, and hobbies. Then it works

15

into abstract queries (kids call them "weird") like "If your family were a noise, what would it be?" or "The color I usually feel like is _____." Answers to these kinds of questions can be very revealing.

So how does this profile help me work with kids? Well, if a child lists English under "least favorite," I begin mapping strategies immediately. Hobbies and interests will give me a clue about changing that attitude. I may try to build rapport by engaging this person in a topic of her interest, or ask that she share her expertise with me in designing something for the room.

Or the profile may suggest other problems need attention first. Scott says the three people he'd most like to meet are Charles Manson, Attila the Hun, and Jack the Ripper. If his family were a sound, it would be like tires squealing; the animal he most resembles is dead; he usually feels black; his hobby is burning cats; and if he could change anything in this world, it would be his parents. He rated his life a "D–" and then crossed it out and made it an "F." How was Scott's summer? Does he want me to ask?

Scott is a ninth grader, so I'd probably have heard before this if he'd had serious problems. Because I've heard nothing of him, I conclude that he is either new to our school or he's had an interesting summer. In any event, his status demands prompt investigation.

Kids can change dramatically during the summer. Some who bounced off walls as eighth graders stride maturely into my ninth-grade classroom, five inches taller and ready to listen. Others have begun to self-destruct: the access to older kids, drugs and alcohol, cars and sex; less parental supervision; a split in the family—many things may have wisened, hardened, or begun wasting the child of three months earlier. The PPS often suggests that this has happened. "My hobbies are parties. My best skill is partying. . . . The thing I would most like to change is the drinking age, curfews, laws, parents."

The Personal Profile Sheet helps me see troubles coming, or at least alerts me to those kids who may need extra encouragement or special attention these first weeks.

Youngsters beginning the year angry, confused, or new to the school may want someone to notice. The PPS gives them a way of inviting my concern.

The PPS enabled me to solicit prompt intervention for Scott: he had fallen deeply into drug use and was in treatment within two weeks.

Doug hated English. I could tell by the !!!! he put after writing "english" in the space after "least favorite subject." He was a large boy and sullen—and had beautiful handwriting skills. Doug's favorite subject was "Art!!!"

I enlisted Doug to pen lettering for my bulletin board— gave him extra credit points—and assured him I'd look forward to his work on the book report projects because some of them could involve drawing. He earned Cs and Bs all year in English.

Information from the PPS has always helped me intervene early with children who never realized I was intervening. And, at the very least, what I learn about the variety of interests, talents, and creative minds I'll be connecting with in the following months excites me.

• If the world were made of food, it would taste like

_____.
. . . garbage . . . pizza with everything on it . . . sweet and sour pork . . . assorted nuts . . . spinach ice cream . . . a jawbreaker . . . anything burnt . . .

• If my family were a noise, it would sound like

_____.
. . . a rock concert . . . a summer morning . . . an earthquake . . . an ape attack . . . an explosion . . . a whisper . . . drums . . . tubas . . . trumpets . . . marbles in a clothes dryer . . .

• My best skill is_____.
. . . talking . . . eating . . . hunting . . . woodworking . . . caring for plants . . . patience . . .

Many teachers think acquiring personal information about kids is a waste of time. I believe that by ignoring kids' jargon and belittling their tastes, we disaffirm the value of youngsters. Of course that invites indifference and erodes our influence with them. To talk and dress like kids is not necessary and can make us look ridiculous. That doesn't mean we can't say, "That color looks good on you, Meg. Did you wear that to the Bon Jovi concert? How was it?" Or "How long have you been trapping, Jack? What does a fox pelt earn these days?"

Kids don't like Mr. Fossile much. "All he does is lecture in that same boring voice. . . . He like knows his subject, but he doesn't know how to get it across." Fred sits in the lounge a lot, complaining about kids—their "attitudes," their language, their music, the way they dress. As for himself, Fred bought two polyester suits in 1972, once he was sure the "no-iron" claim was the real McCoy. He added a pair of plaid pants in '79. Fred thinks Bon Jovi is a flavor of ice cream; he prides himself on being out of date. Fred is from the "old" school, where kids were nearly always re-spectful and could be slapped into line when they weren't. Since he cares little for his "subjects," his subjects care even less for anything he has to say.

"I hate history: Mrs. Flinch thinks reading that book and answering worksheets are the only things I have to do in life. . . . She assigns homework like hers is the only class I'm taking." For all she knows, hers *is* the only class you have. Mrs. Flinch has never seen you any other place. She doesn't know that you swim and take dance and help Thursdays at the nursing home. She has never advised a club, coached, helped with an after-school activity, or chaperoned a dance—anywhere where she could see that kids have other interests. Mrs. Flinch believes hall supervision is too demeaning for someone of her fineness.

Too bad. Assisting colleagues and students in out-of-class functions is an opportunity to show we're good sports. And our help in these activities is appreciated and remembered. It's not so hard to be a good sport about such things, or to decline graciously when we cannot help. "He's not so bad," I heard a student say, defending Mr. Hithertoo. "We asked him at the last minute to supervise the dance and he agreed. Otherwise it would have been canceled."

Investing time with kids and colleagues outside the classroom has always paid me more than I've spent. Knowing I can bank on their support in a tight spot is a reassuring and powerful feeling.

Kids are the most important subjects we teach. Knowing their interests and attitudes, appreciating that they are often pressured and sometimes spread thin outside our classrooms, and understanding something of how each of them thinks is critical insider information.

Simply put, knowledge is power: the more we know about our clients, the better able we are to anticipate their needs and attend to them in ways that will prove sucessful and earn us respect. Strive that first day (and afterward too) to let kids see why you love your job—there is so much variety, so many possibilities, so many opportunities here. Do something fun with them. And use a form of the PPS. Just an hour studying these sheets and you'll be better prepared for each of those kids. Moreover, their responses may remind you, as they do me, of how wide-ranging are kids' interests and skills and values, of how weird and wild and funny and warm kids are, of how much they need our investment in them, and of how filled with possibilities each of them is.

PERSONAL PROFILE SHEET

1. My full name is _____.
2. My birthday is _____.
3. My parents' names are _____.
4. My address is _____.
5. My phone number is _____.
6. I have _____ brothers and _____ sisters.
7. My pets are _____.
8. My hobbies are _____.
9. My favorite subject is _____.
   My least favorite subject is _____.
10. My best skill is _____.
11. If my family were a noise, it would sound like _____.
12. If the world were made of food, it would taste like

    _____.
13. If I could meet three people from the past, they would
    be _____ , _____ , and _____ .
14. The animal I most resemble now is _____.
15. The *smell* that best describes my home is _____.
16. The *color* that best tells how I usually feel is _____.
17. If I could have anything I wanted, it would be _____.
18. The thing I would most like to change in this world is

    _____.
19. If I could live anywhere I liked, I would live in _____.
20. At this point, I would rate my life as follows
    (*Circle one*): A   B   C   D   F
21. Write anything here that would help me understand
    you and work with you better. (This part is optional.)

    _____
    _____.

DAY ONE

Welcome
Enjoy your years at Excalibur Junior High. We have high
expectations for you and you should expect a great deal from
yourself. Set your goals and reach them. If it is going to be,
it is up to you.

This paragraph introduced seven pages of rules to our students their first day of school. Each teacher was to go over these rules with homeroom students during the first week. Expectations from A (Assembly Programs) to T (Textbooks) were defined. The word *should* was used nine times on the first page alone.

I think being "should on" is demeaning, and anyone who has been a parent or a child has experienced the giving or the receiving of much "should." Each of us knows then that even a little is too much. And when not being "should on," these students were told—emphatically: "Enjoy your years . . . Set your goals and reach them." Only the "or else" was missing. I felt the tone of the document was dictatorial and possessed of glacial warmth. I refused to go through it with the kids.

A firm and direct approach is often appropriate. I suspect this "Welcome," however, was modeled after a directive aimed at inmates entering state prison. And for many students this was just the first salvo in a bombardment of rules that day. In fact, under "Classroom Expectations" the master rules sheet says, "Students will receive a statement of classroom rules and regulations from each teacher." Teachers, administrators, and school discipline committees have to do better in "welcoming" kids.

First-day interactions with kids can empower us to enjoy them, to teach them, and to help them acquire legitimate power for themselves. As the shampoo commercial says, "You only get one chance to make a good first impression." Whatever the source, I appreciate a good line and so offer it, and this, for your consideration: These are kids we may see for each of the next 180 school days. Do we really wish to greet them with "dos" and "don'ts" and "shoulds"?

So if not with rules, where to start? Actually, taking roll is not a bad place to begin. I start by writing my name on the board: M-A-H-L-E.

"It's pronounced 'Molly,' like in 'girl.' Names are important. I'm proud of mine and like it to be pronounced correctly. I feel we owe each other that courtesy, so as I call your name, please do correct me if I mispronounce it.

"In addition, some of you like being called a first name other than the one I have listed here. You may come up and tell me now, or just explain when I call your given name. I wish to call you by your preferred name. My name is Mr. Mahle—and that is what I prefer to be called.

"Please show patience with me: I'm an older person and may take longer to learn your names. But I will learn them all, though you may tire of reminding me sometimes."

(Later your legend grows when not one of those kids ever has to give you help with his or her name.)

After going through the roll and penciling in "Shelly" for "Michelle," "Pat" for "Patrick," and changing "Oswald" to "Butch," I talk about myself.

"I have taught here for 15 years. I teach for several different reasons. First of all, I like kids. With kids, every day is different—something creative and interesting is always happening. Secondly, in teaching I can deal with things that excite me. Two things you'll hear a lot about this year are *possibilities* and *power.* I like considering always the various possibilities in things, and I like seeing young people discover the power they have when their minds are opened to possibilities. Let's do an activity."

(I don't know where I found this short poem, but inevitably it provokes thought as students seek for and find a number of possible meanings.)

Argument

Two stubborn beaks
of equal strength
can stretch a worm
to any length.

"In the space below, I'd like you just to sketch briefly what you think is being talked about in this poem. You will not be judged on your drawing: if you are like me, perhaps the best you can do are stick figures. I won't have you hold them up or ask you to show them around, either. Simply sketch what you think is going on in this short piece."

Inevitably, all but two or three students draw birds tugging on worms. I remember those special two or three, then wander about uttering approving grunts. After a minute or two I ask them to draw again.

"Okay, that's great. Now, I'd like you to read the poem again, very carefully. I'd like you then to draw some other possible meaning for this poem. You can draw anything other than what you've already drawn. Don't be afraid to get weird and draw something you'd never have thought a moment ago."

After a minute: "How many of you drew birds this time? How many of you drew birds the first time? Why? Did you think that because it mentioned beaks and worms it had to be about birds? Does it say 'birds'? No. You extended your imagination to believe it was birds because of the images or word pictures that the words *beaks* and *worm* made in your minds. Did any of you not draw birds the first time? Why? What words from the poem suggested something other than birds to you? Are there any such words? Yes. *Stubborn*. Yes. We don't think of birds as stubborn. No. So you drew two people tugging over a sale item in a store. And you drew two people with clouds over their heads saying things that indicate what? Yes. An argument. And you drew soldiers, one holding an American flag and another a Russian flag. Yes. And all of this makes sense, eh? Why? Why do we know this poem cannot be about birds? What is there here that doesn't work for birds but does work for humans? Yes. You simply cannot stretch a worm to any length. It will break. But an idea, a grudge—yes."

This activity does several things. First, it clearly shows kids that thinking will be requisite to learning in this classroom and that they will be much in charge of their own learning. It also introduces my theme of "possibilities," and how those of us who are alert empower ourselves to see more vividly than others. The activity is also fun and focuses on the discipline of learning rather than on the learning of disciplinary rules and jargon.

Of course, not everyone can work a poem into Day One as conveniently as an English teacher. I hope, however, that on the first day you'll involve the kids in the things you enjoy about teaching. Fifteen minutes of this activity leaves me time to explain my one rule (see "Be Appropriate," page 30). Afterward, each student completes the Personal Profile Sheet.

During the first week I take kids through the usual necessaries. They are issued books, given a seating arrangement, given a list of needed materials, and I talk about expectations. I may do one of these things each day. Each student also stands before the class and tells his or her name and mentions three positive things about himself or herself.

Prior to these self-introductions I teach basic speaking techniques: poise, projection, eye contact, and rate. I also explain and then give a quiz on how an audience listens properly. But one need not teach English to instruct kids in ways of speaking and listening properly.

I continue developing the themes of power and possibilities by saying something like this: "Words are our friends when we understand their power and develop the communication skills to use them. That's why I feel it is important that you are able to present yourself in front of the class. Shyness can be crippling and can keep away people who might otherwise be our friends. And word power, or knowing how to ask specifically for things and express our needs, gets the attention of parents and others who can then judge our maturity by what we know. Parents are especially delighted when they believe you are growing up, and they often think they see this when you speak more like an adult; that is, when your requests and discussions seem to be calmly expressed and make sense. Parents truly want to give you more freedom, but they are afraid: they are afraid that you aren't ready, that you don't know enough yet. Word power and the power of self-care impress many people who are then able to grant you more freedom and with that, open you up to a world of wonderful possibilities."

All of this by design establishes a climate of comfort and safety. Kids still don't like presenting themselves, but armed with the knowledge of how it is best accomplished, they succeed, and they begin building their own base of power with their classmates and with me.

We also talk more about "power" and "possibilities" that first week. And finally, begin focusing on individual needs using information gained from the Personal Profile Sheet (see page 20).

Opening day at the ballpark or opening night at the theater—any event that develops and sustains public interest does not begin with a lecture on rules and regulations. Ignore the platitudes of the past: "Don't smile until Christmas. . . . Lay it on the line—If they mess with the bull, give them the horns."

On opening day I allow little chatter and no milling about. I dismiss the class after the bell, and only after they've been silent for any last-second instructions. I lead them out the door (this is the procedure I'll use every day throughout the year), and yes, I don't smile too benignly.

Starting at roll call, however, each student knows that I respect his or her individuality, as I express confidence that each of them will respect mine. Each student knows I like kids, and why I like my job, and that I'll trust them to remember just one rule. We'll have done something together that's a little bit fun. And by day's end they'll remember one class where they were not welcomed as inmates—one class they might, just possibly, look forward to going to the next day.

Rules

—As a faculty we need to agree on some rules and then stick to 'em.

—Yeah, and I think it would be good for these kids if each of us laid it on the line the very first day.

—You bet. Let 'em hear it six times the first day. Then they'll know we mean business.

Enthusiastic support for notions like this—probably at your first faculty meeting—testify to the pervasive sense of powerlessness felt by these teachers. As a rule, hammering kids with rules is a big mistake. Recall your adolescent school experiences.

For me a "rules" list offered a framework for determining the degree of creative mischief I'd bring to that class. Rules inspired me to study which of them I could safely circumvent—knowing the teacher could never enforce them without a brigade of help—and which rules I could follow literally to ludicrous and comic extremes. I had no compunction in this; after all, I was violating a list, not a person.

Besides, in a class where all was spelled out for me, I could best show my cleverness not by following rules but by inventing my own. Rules intimidate shy students, irritate angry students, and encourage bright students to play dumb. And they take the whole first day to explain. And more time later to explain some more:

—Well, Benjamin, I guess you could know that "keep your hands off the windows" meant you weren't to kick them open with your feet.

—Where does it say that, Ms. Sternwheeler?

—That's enough of your smart mouth. . . . I don't want you touching the windows, period.

—I'm sorry. It's just that you didn't say that anywhere.

—Must everything be spelled out in black and white? Besides, I'm saying that now.

—Yes, Ma'am. But what if someone, you know, lets a bad one, you know, makes gas, and the window is closed, and you're way up there and can't smell it, and we get sick here and pass out or maybe throw up or . . . ?

—That will do. No more questions.

—Yes, Ma'am.

Rules. Think about this: if children are so intellectually or socially disadvantaged that they do not know what appropriate behavior is, certainly you can't expect them to read and understand a long list of rules. Especially you can't expect them to read between the lines, to apply higher-level thinking skills and create logical applications or extensions of these rules.

If your kids need a lot of rules, a list won't help. Moreover, a list robs you of power. It says: "Here's what I don't wish to deal with. Pleeeeeease don't make me. Pretty please." And the longer the list, the more you distance yourself from kids, because they soon see you hope to control them more by written commandment than by interaction.

If a student misbehaves, recognize it as inappropriate to a situation; don't refer to the rule against it. Kids need recognition of inappropriate behavior and sometimes seek it in lieu of positive recognition. Still, nonjudgmental confrontation not only affords real opportunities to teach, but it also acknowledges an individual's existence and thus enhances your power base. Remember, only people who know that you esteem their existence can grant you power to guide them.

Finally, by not allowing a list to speak for you, you avoid this purgatory of kids' thoughts about rules:

—How dumb does she think I am?
—Whaaaaaat?
—He has got to be kidding.
—This sucks.
—This is going to be fun.

And from the gifted,

—If you can't see I'm capable of caring for myself, don't expect *me* to. And if you do see I'm bright, don't expect me to show you by expanding logically from your list to create even more rules that might later be used against me.

Every classroom needs structure, order, a sense of purpose. But teachers err badly when they hope lists of rules will accomplish these things. Leadership will make these things happen; you know this from your own school experiences. Your best teachers did not stand behind lists of rules. Rules? You only need one.

"Be Appropriate."

"My name is Mr. Mahle. I have one rule for this classroom. That's right, one rule, so listen carefully. The rule is,'Be appropriate'." (I give kids a moment to digest this, to share a knowing grin with their friends as they think briefly of the havoc they'll enjoy with so few rules to control them.) "Now I know all of you understand what 'appropriate' is. I can see that because each of you is at this moment behaving appropriately. You are sitting quietly, somewhat anxiously perhaps, wondering about this guy with the strange-sounding rule—the one that suggests to some of you that I might put up with anything." (Grinners now listen even more intently.) "Of course you are right, bright persons that you are. I will put up with anything I feel is appropriate.

"For you who are confused a bit, 'appropriate' means you do what the situation calls for, as you're doing now by listening quietly. 'Appropriate' may on some occasion mean laughing, or getting up, moving around, talking to friends. But now it means listening quietly, and I'm so pleased each of you understands that. If some of you were mentally handicapped or crazy, I'd see that already and know who would need special instruction in understanding what 'appropriate' means. I'm very pleased that each of you is perfectly in control. That's good—none of you is crazy. I like that.

"Of course, some kids like to be crazy, or to let the teacher think they are. Crazy kids get away with a lot. It can be really fun acting nuts. But I make allowances only for legitimate insanity. So if one or two of you had intentions of maybe later trying to convince me you're crazy, you've lost that chance. You needed to start bouncing off walls the moment you came in. Sorry. It's too late now for that. So if later you decide to be crazy . . . well, I'll know you made a choice to be that way, or else something new I'll want to know about has happened in your life to make you that way.

"It's good we can all understand these things right now, this first day. This is going to be a great class."

Yes, you will have to remind kids of what is appropriate for your classroom, but most already know: they know by your confident, nonthreatening tone, by the insight you have into the "crazy" games kids like to play, and by the positive strokes you gave in recognizing the control they have already shown.

This approach has several advantages over more traditional opening days wherein students are besieged with a blizzard of handouts listing more dos and don'ts than they could forget in a full term.

First, this approach empowers the teacher—rather than empowering a sheet of rules—with responsibility for guiding student behavior.

Second, this approach reduces the number of arguable rules to zero. What sane arguments can be raised against requiring that students behave appropriately?

Third, this approach erases some of the "gotcha" games kids play with spell-it-out-to-the-dummies type rules. ("But it says to keep hands off the windows, Ms. Sternwheeler. Don't say nothin' about usin' feet.")

With lists, anything requiring broad interpretation invites circumvention or playing dumb. The teacher must then explain, usually at the expense of valuable lesson time. Because getting you to digress was probably their main purpose in testing the rule, any discussion rewards the perpetrators.

Fourth, students can now secure legitimate power for themselves by making laudable behavioral choices instead of following a tedious list of dos and don'ts. Individually and collectively, they are already exhibiting social responsibility and experiencing self-esteem. Be certain you notice then:

"I've had classes that wouldn't have worked quietly so long on their own in the library. . . . This class certainly understands how to respect the rights of others. . . . Each of you seems to know how to deliver mature behavior."

"You didn't treat us like little kids." When students evaluate my classroom management this way at the end of the year, it's because I've been able to delegate power. By insisting they make thoughtful decisions about what is appropriate, I've offered my students opportunities for gaining self-assurances and enabled them to expand their repertoires of useful behaviors. They appreciate that.

Of course, like us, kids will sometimes make poor choices. But when we guide, model, and praise—in short, when we *teach*—kids will mostly choose well. When they don't, think of it not as an affront—unless it is—but as an opportunity to better do this job, part of which is to point out the consequences of poor choices and to encourage the discovery of the better alternatives available to *thinking* people. That's right. This single simple rule demands that kids think. All year long, kids will make discerning choices about what is and what is not okay. Kids thinking—kids being empowered to think—that's power teaching.

"You Get to . . ."

—Oh Mister Maaaaahhhhleeee, do we haaaavvve to
read this whooooole booooook, eeehhhhhvry chapter?
And do aaaall the stuff on this sheeeeeet we went over?
Do we haaavvvve to? Do we? Huh? Do we?
—No.
—What? We don't? We don't have to do aaaany of this?
—No.
—You mean we pick out whatever we want to do?
—No.
—You mean we doooo haaaave to do it—all of it?
—No, you don't haaaave to. You geeeet to.
—We get to? That's what you meant—we *get* to?
—That's right—that's the ticket. Now you catch on?
—So what? Have to, get to—it's the same thing.

It's not the same thing, of course. "Get to" implies
privilege and reward, and I assert that education is most
effectively received when delivered wrapped in that attitude.
Kids like to believe that anything we ask them to do is
punitive. Indeed, why shouldn't they? After all, they are
compelled to be in school. It's important, therefore, that we
separate ourselves philosophically from the law that forces
their attendance.

Learning is a privilege. Kids need that communicated
by our examples: our eagerness to learn from them, our
own reading, our attendance at workshops, our interest in
the world around us, the newspaper on our desk, magazines on the spare table, our vibrant and ever-changing
bulletin boards. But mostly, kids need to see our esteem for
education reflected in excitement for sharing what we know
and for exploring new territories with them—and especially

in our resolve not to use education, or the tasks commonly connected with it, as punishment.

"Okay, you people chose not to read Chapter 1 for today. Tonight you'll have that chapter and 2 and 3 as well and a test on all three tomorrow." Message? Reading this book must be something asked of people you are upset with.

> —This is your third time late, Willie. You'll write 500 times "I, Willie Loman, will not be late to English again." Before you can come into this room, you'll have that done.
> —I, Willie . . . what?

I sometimes use writing to encourage kids to reflect on their behaviors, to explain why they did or did not behave a certain way, or to suggest alternatives they might have chosen. Mindlessly repeating an excruciating exercise may move Willie to find my room on time, but it won't build his esteem for the writing process. There is a profound difference between writing as punishment and writing for the purpose of delineating and reflecting on behavior.

The good-natured banter I shared earlier with that student (the one we've all had many times, who whines, "Do we haaaave to?") works. As the year winds on, this same child will answer his own question with his own good-natured "I know—we *get* to."

I never force kids to do work: sometimes they are urged along by vivid images of what the consequences for not doing work may be, but always they can choose not to do school work.

> —What if we don't do this, Mr. Mahle? What will happen then?
> —Nothing.
> —What? You mean I can *not* do this book report and nothing will happen?
> —Exactly. Nothing, zilch, zero.

—OOOhhhh, I get it—zero. I'll get a zero for the assignment.

—Well, when I get to the place in my grade book for your score on this assignment—the same column where I've been writing in 15s and 20s for the other kids—like I said, when I get to your space, nothing will happen.

—Very funny. So I can choose not to do this, but I'll fail.

—Nothing will happen: you'll learn nothing, you'll earn nothing.

—And then I'll fail and you'll have to call my parents and I'll be grounded for life.

—And?

—And I'll have to repeat ninth grade and all my friends will go on to high school without me and I'll never get into a good college or get a good job and my life will be ruined.

—Is that how it works?

—Yes.

—Wow! Would you like some help then in organizing your report?

Keeping things simple, matter-of-fact, pushes kids away from the adversarial role they sometimes enjoy as a way of reacting to their compulsory attendance. We are not the enemy. We teach because we enjoy kids and ideas. Kids learn when they enjoy teachers and ideas. We share ourselves in ways that show we love learning. We extend ourselves to kids, offering strategies and skills and techniques that will empower them to eventually learn on their own.

We don't have time to justify every task we ask of students, to argue "what ifs," to righteously extol the virtues of learning. Indeed, we quietly assert that *getting* to do something is happier than *having* to do it, and that consequently, most students would rather do something than nothing.

KNOW YOUR TURF

As a beginning teacher I was advised to first make the acquaintance of the custodial staff. Along with a key to the faculty lavatory, nothing was more essential for a beginning teacher's quest for peace of mind. I did as advised. I introduced myself to Clem and commented on the terrific appearance of the building—and of my room specifically. I took time every morning to chat with custodians during those first teacher-workshop days.

On the first day of school, my fourth class was busily filling out personal profile sheets when a tall boy anxiously approached my desk and asked for a lavatory pass. I wrote it quickly, handed it to him, and he proceeded toward the door, pausing long enough only to vomit in the entryway. It was near dismissal time—I suppose he'd thought he could hold back—and soon 30 kids would be leaving and 30 more entering through the remnants of this youngster's first school lunch.

I called the office immediately, requested help from Clem—an emergency—and he arrived in minutes, mopping the last of the mess just as class dismissed. I've never since had a kid vomit in class, so in retrospect I know the incident was initiated by inexplicable cosmic forces to impress upon me the wisdom of knowing the custodial staff.

No force in your school can more conveniently support or thwart your efforts to establish teaching power. These folks silence buzzing lights, whining clocks, and fresh air vents whistling with pencil bits and sucker sticks. They replace voracious pencil sharpeners, dead fluorescents, and broken desks. They open your locked classroom door after someone has broken pencil lead in the lock, rendering your key useless. And yes, each of them has a master key and can let you in where you need to go when you've left your keys at home.

Knowing your turf also means knowing who there can assist you in times of real need. Know the office secretary by name, the school nurse (and where she is), and the counselors. Know the cooks and where you can get a projector (or a bulb for one) and who can quickly type a test for you. And, if there is time, know your principal too.

Of course it's good to know as many colleagues as you can, most essentially those on either side of you and across the hall. Know your colleagues' free periods and where they hang out then. Could they help you a moment should you suddenly be seized with colic during an explanation of participles?

Learn who the specialists are in the building—those who teach and work with students who are hearing impaired, learning disabled, emotionally disturbed, mentally handicapped—because you'll soon need their expertise in selecting effective strategies for kids. Know your counselors; they have insights into why some kids are difficult and can help arrange conferences with parents if necessary. Counselors are an invaluable resource.

Learn all you can about the building, where the lavatories are, and the science classrooms and the band room Johnny always comes late from. Is it really located across town? Or does Johnny stop in the lobby to meet friends? Know where things are stored in case you need a mop some time.

Knowing your turf can bolster your power base. Know what rooms near you are empty and when. Know if you can use them in a pinch—to let a child make up a test, for instance, or for time out to think. Know what distractions may exist between the student and the empty room, such as a fire alarm, a fire extinguisher, a drinking fountain, a lavatory, or other occupied rooms. Where is the nearest phone? (Every room should have a phone: if you want to lobby for a cause that would greatly facilitate your use of time, lobby for phones.) Know how to use a fire extinguisher and how to contact the office for information or help in a moment.

If you have windows, know how they open and close and what's outside them. For years I've taught in rooms with windows through which an acrobatic youngster could reach a small ledge. Some have.

Know what is below your windows. When a fire started in my overhead projector last year, I was able to dislodge the burning material harmlessly to the loading dock below. But that loading dock can cause terrible distractions if I'm not prepared, for nearly every item coming into the building is delivered there, and garbage is picked up daily. I can anticipate outside noise and plan accordingly.

Know how to use equipment to facilitate teaching. That means slide projectors, overhead projectors, film projectors, tape recorders, VCRs—all of it. A colleague and I shared the same room for three years. Many times she'd come in and ask, "What film did you show? Did the kids enjoy it? Did it make the point you wanted it to?"

"Yes," I'd answer.

"Someday I'll just have to show a film."

She never did, even though we taught the same subject, the same units. Her kids soundly protested that they were being cheated—they probably were—but she never used that resource. "I'm so afraid it will burn up, or the kids will sabotage the thing, or . . ."

Through incidents of avoidance, her powerlessness became evident to students, and though she was bright, good-natured, caring, and competent in many other respects, some kids saw her as weak, and they treated her meanly. How simple just to have had someone teach her use of the machine—to rehearse the threading and starting and focusing. I don't know why she wouldn't ask for help. Pride? Stubbornness? Or ignorance of the impact video media can make on less-verbal students? No matter, for she doesn't teach anymore. I can't help wondering though what power base she brings to other relationships—with family, husband, friends; with lawn mowers, digital watches, word processors.

Finally, knowing your turf means knowing your room. Know the cold spots and warm spots; know the condition of every desk and wall. Know the only place you keep chalk, erasers, and the room wastebasket. Command your turf like you would your own home. Have it in order when kids arrive, and insist on seeing it returned to order when each class leaves. They can pick up paper, they can straighten desks, they can refrain from doodling on the desk and walls. But they need to know you regard it as your turf, that you know its quirks and advantages well, and that they are welcome guests there for as long as they treat it right.

Walk about the room often, proudly, comfortable in the space. Kids sense your ease and are happy then to be comfortable with you. Moreover, they are reluctant to deface what you take pride in; instead, most will help decorate bulletin boards with their own best work. Thank them for it, and for helping maintain neatness, and for respecting your work place, your turf.

PART II

Strategies for Maintaining Your Power

LET THEM
WONDER A BIT

My sixth-grade teacher, Mrs. Hanson, had several
weaknesses. First of all, she had a fierce temper and
confronted insolence with abrupt, righteous indignation
that many of us found amusing, once we learned it was all
just thunder. Secondly, she was hugely good-hearted and
couldn't maintain even a pout much longer than a minute
after the original eruption. The storm would subside and
the rainbow would appear—an apology and usually a
reduction or even a retraction of the penalty, depending on
the offender's capacity for mustering an injured look. She
was a good person, and we exploited her at every
opportunity.

Mrs. Hanson, you see, was totally predictable. I can
still see her with her back to us, writing on the board, then
jerking around like a wounded bear at the sound of Tom's
great green jumbo eraser hitting the venetian blinds. Off
came the glasses, and her eyes, as though thrust out by
the centrifugal force of her spin, began scoping the room,
scrinching at the faces most distant, bugging again as she
surveyed the closer kids, seeking out a smirk that would
indict the offender.

Whoever it was, or whoever she determined it was,
would be dispatched directly to the hall with an elegant,
swirling hand gesture (and be recalled a few minutes later
after a cool-down during which she'd be heard to mutter,
"I'm not giving up on that boy.") It was always a boy, and
usually Larry if she wasn't sure, which was okay since he
got away with plenty anyway.

Well, the point is not to be always predictable,
especially not to convulse over every offense. Kids wonder
what you'll do in a real crisis if you flounder over the first
thing tossed your way. (Don't ignore it, of course, but make

an appointment: "Larry, we'll talk a minute after class.") We
liked the old gal, but we had her pegged too early.

Often when kids are beginning to like you, they
evidence this by wanting to know things about your
personal life. "How old are you, anyhow? . . . Really? We
thought you were older." "Do you have kids? . . . Oooow,
those poor kids. I hope they don't look like you . . . just
kidding."

—What's your first name?
—Mister.
—Aw, c'mon. Tell us your first name.
—I told you, it's "Mister"—my kids call me "Mister."
—Yeah, sure. What does your wife call you?
—I can't say that with so many young people around.
—C'mon, what's your first name? I know. I'll ask Mrs.
Fern. She'll tell me.
—No she won't.
—Well, there's other ways to find out.
—That's true—like maybe looking at the label on any of
those magazines stacked on the table back there.
—Hey. I'll check it out.
—Never mind, it's "Benjamin."
—Benjamin—Benjie—do your friends call you "Benjie"?
—Some of them, and my mother.
—What if we called you Benjie?
—I wouldn't like that very well.
—Why not?
—You're not my mother.

A former colleague encouraged students to call her by
her first name. She thought it brought them closer. Maybe
it did. She was deeply loved, or hated, by those kids, for
many were moved to regard her as they did their peers. She
hugged a lot and shouted, even exchanged epithets, and
felt the airing was healthy.

It wasn't for her—she broke down with the burden of too many emotions—too many kids wanting, begging, demanding too much. It was a tragic loss, a caring teacher without the tools to build a career that would go the distance—not a year, or five, or ten—a career. We need tools to take us all the way, in style, to exit with our health and power for the next phase.

We can be friendly with kids; we can even be friends, I've found, but not in the casual way kids are friends with their peers. A certain distance must be maintained to ensure credibility, respect, power.

Adolescents see themselves as uncertain, searching, awkward. Though they will try to reduce us to that too, they don't really want us there. So we need to operate at their level of language and comprehension and to be caring and available to listen—but in the status of competent, confident adults. Otherwise, kids will treat us like one of their own. Ever notice how kids treat each other, even their friends?

I always go through the first-name thing, and some-times I just tell them right out. But I like the under-standing, gently but firmly expostulated, that I prefer to be called "Mister." A first-name basis is reserved for family and adult friends, colleagues.

Kids want to get close, to be familiar, and sometimes they need such an adult when none exists elsewhere for them. It's a temptation—especially for you who care so much—but stay back a bit. Personal knowledge is power, as we know, and although I trust teachers to use personal knowledge in the best interests of their students, I am not so trustful of kids. Be careful how you answer the question "Did you ever smoke dope?" And never, never, never answer that kind of question about a colleague.

"No, I don't smoke dope. Do I act like someone who smokes dope, or why would you ask?" Most of the time that smoke screen—sorry about that—successfully defers answering the real question. If not, I can be honest—"I tried it once or twice in college"—knowing that with kids "in college" bestows pardon for any fad or prank they can imagine. It's probably safer, though, just to lie: "No. Why do you suppose they call it 'dope'?"

We teach subjects, we teach a subject, and we are sometimes the subjects under scrutiny. That's okay. In all cases, it's good that questions are asked. The value may be in the asking, the mental fidgeting that begs to know who, what, where, why, how. It's okay to be something of an abstraction, for there is a power—as well as an appealing mystery—in ambiguity. And it's okay to be very clear about some things, like how you expect to be addressed.

It's not a game, but rather an attitude about what students might reasonably be allowed to know about you. It's not a contest, but rather your right to ignore, misinterpret, deny, or redirect personal directives.

"EXCUSE ME, BUT . . ."

"Excuse me" is a powerful disarmer. Students are caught off guard—especially if they've been inappropriate—when you grab their attention with an apology. At this point, slip them the message.

—Excuse me, but since you came in late, I know you'll not want to distract the class further by talking to Jake.

—Excuse me, but since those scraps on the floor are from your papers, I know you'll not expect someone else to pick them up.

—Excuse me, but since you kids would probably rather not have this work to do tonight, I know you'll want to get started now on today's lesson.

The more assertive form of "excuse me" is "I beg your pardon."

—I beg your pardon, but if you can explain how throwing spit wads improves learning in this classroom, I'll be glad to listen to you after school tonight.

—I beg your pardon, but if you would like to explain to Johnny's parents why he should have to be called names by you, I'll be glad to arrange the interview.

Rarely are these "apologies" challenged. People are not conditioned to challenge apologies. Of course these are not really apologies, but cues about how to clean up one's behavior. Still, kids treat this approach with respect if your tone is assertive but nonparental and nonjudgmental. Above all, avoid sarcasm. The key to sustained success using this technique, however, comes in following with a specific alternative to the undesired behavior.

We can arrange interviews, we can assign homework, we can expect kids to clean up their messes. Kids know these things are reasonable and right. Soon they learn that when they hear "Excuse me," they're going to get good information.

In this instance we are all-powerful. Our offers to discuss issues raised by this approach are never at the time-expense of the class; we make this clear by the words "after school" or "later." If we deliver our apologies politely, they seldom provoke insolent responses. If they do, humor may lighten the message—an exaggerated "Well, excuuuuuse me!"—or we can feign deafness, noting only if our suggestions are followed. If they are not, we then deal with defiance.

But this technique seldom provokes insolence or defiance. Unlike authoritarian, macho remonstrations like "Clean up that mess!" apologies answer, rather than beg, the question "Or what?"

"That's Not Fair!"

Kids love to attack us with claims of unfairness. If we don't treat everyone and each situation the same, we are open to this criticism. That's good. Kids, after all do not want fairness; they want justice. They want us to be flexible when they've been stiffed by circumstance. Then we are entitled to make judgments that consider their special needs.

Many teachers don't want to do this. "A rule is a rule," and that works for them—to a degree. However, my one rule, "Be appropriate," applies to teachers too. I may well give Jenny an extra day for her assignment when she explains how her weekend swim meet in Fargo didn't give her time to read the story and answer the questions I assigned Friday. I am not likely to give her an extra day, however, if the assignment was a book report assigned four weeks ago.

If I doubt the accuracy of a student's claim, I may ask the student to bring a note from a parent or counselor explaining why additional time is needed for the assignment. That is not an unreasonable request, and it clearly discourages the whining procrastinator from enjoying the same privileges as the well-intentioned person caught short of time by more important issues. If I'm not acquainted well enough with a student to know the score, I would proceed this way:

—I'm sure your swimming is very important to you, Jenny, and I know it demands a lot of time. Still, it's a long drive to Fargo. Couldn't you have done some reading on the way?

—I get sick when I read in the car.

—I see. Well, I'd like to give you another day for this work. The problem I have is that all the other kids had

to turn in the work today. It would help if you'd bring a note in with your assignment—something from Mom or Dad explaining how you really had no time to fit the reading and writing in over the weekend. Okay?
—I guess.
—Good. It needn't be a long note—just a few lines. And next time you know you'll be gone, if you tell me beforehand, I can give you the work ahead of the others so that we'll all be able to go over it at the same time.
—Okay. I can do that.

Occasionally, students use their involvement in outside activities to justify doing less in school. Some parents, steeped in pride of their child's accomplishments, may facilitate this behavior. Most I've dealt with do not. Asking for a note from the parents following a first incident like the one above helps me see if they will be partners with me in holding their child accountable for schoolwork. This early contact connecting parent, child, and teacher empowers me with knowing what kind of parent I'm dealing with.

Parents are usually our allies in holding kids accountable. Parents also want reasonable treatment for their kids, and yes, some things outside of class are more important than a particular assignment. Teachers know what is reasonable and need to make decisions accordingly. When teachers make reasonable allowances for students' out-of-school activities, both kids and parents discern an increased power in the teacher's position—power that comes from flexibility.

Early in the school year I state that I'll not promise to be fair. It doesn't take much planning for that opportunity to speak to me. Usually this happens with seating arrangements:

Carla and Debbie are best friends. When, during the second day of class, I'm distracted for the second time by their whispering and move them to opposite sides of the room, Carla groans, "That's not fair. Joan and Judy were whispering too, and you didn't move them." She may be right. No matter. Carla's decision to continue whispering—this was not the first time, and she'd been cautioned earlier—is inappropriate regardless of the choices made by Joan, Judy, Debbie, or anyone she might point to in trying to justify her behavior. It is good to explain this to her after class.

At the moment, though, the "fairness" issue is bouncing like a pinball, turning on lights in every kid's mind. How would you respond here? Try answering in the space provided, in about 100 words, or less. My response follows.

_____

_____

_____

_____

_____

_____

_____

_____

"Thank you, Carla, for mentioning the fairness thing. Kids sometimes think they want life to be fair, but really, most of them don't—especially you kids. Heck, if life were fair, you'd have to give half of what you own to the beggars in India or to the starving folks in Africa—or to me. That's one reason I never promise to be fair. It's too hard to keep track of who owes what to whom. If we each just respect one another's rights to listen and learn, things will seem fair for the most part, I think."

Remember: when we've been reasonable, kids are not likely to applaud or cheer or demonstrate like they do when we appear to be unfair. But they remember. And, eventually, most kids need some special allowance. Though there is some danger in our flexibility being stretched and weakened by manipulative students, a quick call home can confirm suspicions, or, as I've often discovered, prove the student right and worthy of our trust. Otherwise, we risk this:

—Jan, you're late.

—I have a pass from Mrs. Sheridan.

Jan is in a special program for students at risk of failing ninth grade, and Mrs. Sheridan is Jan's behavior-management teacher. I know Jan is a smoker, is frequently tardy to other classes, and is often truant. She is otherwise very likeable, never rude or abusive, and occasionally even friendly. But the pass looks like Jan's writing. Having once been a smoker, I'd often inveigled time away from the work-place to "get one in." I was sure of her deceit.

—You wrote this pass yourself.

—I did not! You can even call Mrs. Sheridan!

—I'll do that right after class.

I did check later: Jan had been telling the truth. In wrongly accusing kids, especially those who are often rightly accused, we evoke a tidal wave of righteous indignation. Since these kids rarely have both truth and their peers as allies, expect them to press that advantage.

I was soundly crushed. Even worse, any openness and trust between Jan and me was unequivocally gone. Previously, she'd even done passing work for me, but after this, nothing. So she may have forged a pass. Big deal. I could have quietly checked with her teacher later. No. I'd had that set-things-straight-right-here-and-now urge—an urge I think we're wise to resist. (See "Hey, You!", pages 67–70 for another instance.)

Now I'd not only been unfair, I'd been unjust. Kids are slow to forget injustice, and an entire class had witnessed my error.

We have the power to be "just," though it sometimes takes checking and can initially be more trouble than just treating everyone the same. To claim you will always be fair, however, is to shackle yourself with an impossible task. You are sure to renege on the claim—usually in the interest of justice—and erode your power base while awkwardly trying to explain why you broke the rules.

Parents as Allies

Psychologist Ray McGee, a popular workshop presenter on the subject of humanizing schools, says that parenting is the most difficult job in the world, and the most terrifying job to fail at. My daughter, at age 3, avenged a teasing from her 10-year-old brother by applying her wooden hammer to his recent collection of baby toads, mashing them on the picnic table. (The stains are still visible today.) I was certain then we'd raised a monster.

As a kindergartener she skipped school one morning and was found by her mother sitting under a tree in our front yard. Upon her forced return to class, she kicked her teacher in the shins—a defiance that drew sobs from her mom. That summer, the child defecated in the flower bed. Now, at 12 she's appalled that I've written these things and denies they could have happened.

Though these things seemed monstrous at the time, I don't recall responding to my daughter as though she were a monster. It is important that parents and teachers not treat kids as monsters even when we think they've behaved that way. When the facts are known, we've usually exaggerated the seriousness of the offense. Still, I've known no hollowness to chill my insides like believing I've failed as a parent.

Parents and teachers are mostly on the same side. When a child fails in the classroom, teachers want to know why. Chances are good that his or her parents are simultaneously concerned with the child's failures at home. There can be many reasons, including the possible impact of inappropriate behaviors by parents or teachers, and even then teachers and parents need to explore the possibilities together. These contacts frequently result in alliances and discovery of helpful strategies. Rarely have I felt myself an adversary of the parent, and never have I found parents indifferent to the problems of their children.

School-sponsored open houses and parent-teacher conferences often enlist parents as allies. Happy-o-grams— letters home noting student achievement or improvement— are popular with parents and students, as are phone calls: "Your daughter helped a seventh grader find his homeroom this first day. . . . Your son offered to tutor a classmate. . . . Bob picked up assignments for a sick friend." These communiqués are gladly received. For a child with a history of making bad decisions, any of these behaviors, or even a choice to stay out of trouble, may be noted and called or mailed home. "Catch kids being good," suggests Ray McGee. Yes. And when we do, it's a great opportunity to connect in a positive way with parents.

It's unfortunate when our first parental contact concerns a child's negative behavior or poor progress at school. But because this is often the case, a tactful approach can still enlist parental support.

My first contact with parents usually concerns their child's academic behaviors. Although not so positive as a happy-o-gram, this call is less threatening than one made about bad behavior. And parents invariably appreciate knowing when their child is achieving below potential.

"Mrs. Jensen? This is Mr. Mahle, Jane's English teacher here at Jefferson. Can you talk for a moment? . . . Good. Since beginning with Jane a week ago, I've been unable to coax any work from her. Could you tell me if she usually begins the year slowly? Her test scores show she has better-than-average ability, and she's told me the material is not confusing for her. Could you give me any insights on how I might urge her to do better?"

Prior to contacting parents I like to research the student's file and talk with counselors and former teachers. This often helps if the parents ask for my suggestions. From my research and observations of the child, I will have several strategies in mind.

"Does Jane watch a lot of television? Could she be motivated to do homework or read a book for an hour each night prior to watching her favorite shows?

"Would Jane be helped by being made accountable for each day in class? I have a prepared form I've used with other kids. I merely indicate 'okay' or 'not okay' with regard to effort and behavior, and sign it."

Familiarity with her file may help me anticipate the existence of family problems. When the conversation indicates a family in need of help, it's valuable then to have the name and number of the child's counselor, along with assurances that this person can direct the parents to specific family services. Sometimes I'll offer to contact the school counselor for them.

Often, parents don't know help is available. Some are aware but held back by fear, pride, or, especially at the beginning of a school year, a hope that the child has somehow changed since last year. It is singularly vital then that we study kids carefully the first few weeks.

Parents like us more when they are told soon after we observe their child lagging. Allowing a child time to rally before contacting the folks, however, sometimes results in immediate improvement. Often the child is thankful for a chance to avoid parental confrontation and rewards you with steady efforts. Give the child a week to show improvement, but be willing then to call home, because the stalling game may reflect a pattern for this child that has worked previously with soft-hearted teachers—and that has exasperated his or her parents. One week maximum for academic improvement is reasonable. After that it's right to phone home.

Since active, positively involved students tend to misbehave less than students disenchanted with learning, enlisting parental cooperation in urging achievement frequently prevents nuisance behavior. Moreover, a child's academic achievement—or lack of it—is more easily documented and less subject to interpretation than are other behaviors. So when do I call about other types of inappropriate, or "nuisance," behaviors?

Actually, I've rarely had to call home to remediate these; other techniques are usually effective, especially the promise—not the threat—to call home if changes are not soon forthcoming. Calling home about bad conduct is a trump card to be used judiciously. The student must realize he or she has been offered every reasonable chance. It's imperative that teachers not make the mistake of "tattling."

Major offenses, such as fighting or smoking, that mandate a child be sent to the vice principal usually result in a call made from that office. The daily annoyances are the ones with which we most often struggle. Sometimes the suggestion of parental involvement is enough to correct minor indiscretions (and very large offenses too, as I'll show later).

Nasty language, having been popularized by all media, is a blight among adolescents. Though such language has its place in context, that context is rarely my classroom. I confront nastiness at every opportunity, for invariably, tolerating or being intimidated by cursing or racial epithets suggests that either I'll allow more or that I'm naive and don't know what I'm hearing. We are often supposed to be ignorant of the latest insults and sexual jargon—and too often we are—and students will test us for that. If we fail, we're targets for more. It's important that we study up (see "Know Your Subjects," pages 15–20), for our power will erode in derision if students believe they know so much more than we. Most often, however, kids test to discover how much we'll abide. The following example happened only a few desks away from me. Both students knew I was within hearing.

—Fred, let me borrow your pencil.
—No. You'll keep it.
—I will not—c'mon, I'll be in trouble without a pencil again today.
—That's your problem.
—It's going to be your problem if you don't lend me one.
—Go buy one.
—C'mon. Lend me one of yours.

—Forget it.
—Well, – – – k you then.

This student knows he's been inappropriate. Moreover, several students who've heard him know that I've heard too. How would you respond to this situation? Write your dialogue below. Try to stay under 150 words. My response follows.

_____
_____
_____
_____
_____
_____
_____
_____
_____
_____
_____
_____
_____
_____
_____
_____

I keep a supply of pencils handy. Following his last comment, I'll lend one to the student. This evokes one of two responses:

"Thanks," he says quietly, soberly in reaction to my straight face. He's saying, "Thanks for not making an issue of my screw-up; I see you're a good guy."

Or he says, "Thanks, teach." This offering, delivered through a wry grin, says, "Thanks for giving me the chance to show my daring; I see you're a wimp."

The first response may reflect the student's belief that I know he was speaking in anger—that I understand this behavior in kids and so forgive him, good guy that I am.

Still, I'll want to speak with him after class so that he'll know such language will be challenged.

The second response is a promise that more tests will be forthcoming.

My next response is vital. All who are within earshot must know that this kind of language will be confronted. But now is not the time for dramatic remonstration. I avoid the urge to "set everything right, right now" and say instead, "You're welcome. After class, when we talk, you can return it to me." Everyone now knows that inappropriate language will be challenged, probably on their time. The young man is no longer swaggering in his seat. After class:

—Of course I heard your response to Fred. Tell me, who taught you to speak to people that way—your father or your mother?

Believe me: kids do not like naming one parent or the other in response to this question.

—Well, what makes you think I learned it at home?

Typically this response indicates that kids believe their behavior does sometimes reflect on their parents, and they are embarrassed. The true degree of parental influence becomes apparent then when he rushes to separate his folks from the inappropriate behavior.

—Then neither Mom nor Dad encourages you to talk like that?
—No. It won't happen again.

In rare cases, the student will accuse one parent or the other. This may be an attempt to seem tough, it may indicate curiosity about my next move, or it may be the truth.

—I find that hard to believe, but I won't call you a liar. I can find out easily enough. In any case, I'm sure your father will be interested in knowing you've identified him as the cause of your problem here.

Swearing, racial epithets, and nasty language do not usually merit immediate calls to parents. If confrontation is answered with defiance, however, I won't hesitate. If it were my kid behaving that way, I'd want to know.

Bob endured frequent verbal harassment from several of the macho boys in our eighth-grade class. I patrolled his area frequently and so discouraged much of the teasing. And disapproving glances tempered the cruelty of his less-vigorous tormentors. But Dave and Bill were relentless and disgusting in tone and gesture, although they were careful to keep the volume below my range of receptivity. I quietly asked Bob what they were telling him. He didn't want to say. I wrestled with the notion of intervening on his behalf, forbidding the other boys any discourse at all. Bob was aghast that I'd do this. "It will only make it worse when you're not around." I'm sure he was right. Dave and Bill were totally insensitive, conscienceless in this matter.

One day I stepped briefly from the room, left the door open, and heard Dave say, "Bob, will you suck mine after school too?" I had long known Bob was being teased about his sexuality—adolescents frequently taunt others this way with name-calling but stop short of referring to specific sexual behaviors. I returned to the room and offered Dave a glare that told him, "This time I heard you." It was enough for the moment. I had next hour free and would act then.

After checking the office for Dave's next scheduled class, I contacted his teacher via room phone and explained that I wanted to talk to Dave about an incident the previous hour—could he be excused for that? I'd be by to get him.

In the empty hallway outside Dave's math classroom I asked him, "What did you say to Bob last hour? He looked uncomfortable when I came back in the room."

—It was nothing. We kid around a lot like that.
—Like what?

—You know—we say stuff to each other.
—What did you say this time?
—Just . . . stuff.
—Okay, enough games. This is what I heard. (I repeat Dave's words.) Explain what you meant by that.

A long pause. His chin probes his chest.

—You'd rather not say.
—No.
—Then I'll explain something to you. I've seen you and Bill harass Bob every time you thought you could. I offered to step in and shut you up, but Bob wouldn't allow it. Do you understand what I'm saying?
—I think so.
—Yes. Bob didn't want me fighting his battles. I respect him a lot for that. But that trash today—no one has to listen to such stuff. Your insinuations surely hurt Bob. And there's only one way you could know the truth of them, isn't there? I hoped you'd grow up and stop on your own. Since you haven't, this is how things are. You don't want to explain what you said to Bob. Fine. But the next time you say anything to him, you'd best be willing to explain it, because if you bother him again, I'm going to call your parents and his parents together, with you and Bob and myself—and we'll all sit down together while you explain what you said to Bob this afternoon. Your parents and his parents, you and I and Bob—we'll all have a little chat together and see if we agree that your comments are as entertaining as you and Bill seem to think they are.

Dave was appropriately humbled, mortified by the image of exposing his vileness to a collection of very interested adults. He and Bill were visibly changed by imagining how their behaviors would be perceived by a powerful and concerned adult alliance. Bob enjoyed the change. And two youngsters in need of a kick got it.

I remember a similar need. At that same age I joined a friend in ridiculing a younger boy who'd worn work shoes to a junior high dance. A better friend took me aside: "Those aren't just Tom's 'dancing shoes' as you called them—those are his only shoes. He mowed a lot of lawns to pay for them, and for that new shirt and pants too, you can bet. His is a big family, you know, and no dad."
I remember.

And I remember with gratitude those who gave the kicks. More than once I was glad to be "kicked" by teachers, rather than to be shamed in front of my parents. Had I spoken to Dave's parents, he would surely have been shamed, would have hated me, and probably Bob, for life. But had he once again spoken disparagingly to Bob, I'd have done as threatened. Dave knew I'd been reasonable in coming first to him. And he knew I was right in promising to use the ace trump if he messed up again.

Some kids' mouths ought to flush when they open them. And we hate dealing with that. Some kids say such things that we want to slap them silly. For the most part, though, such stuff is normal and doesn't show them to be monsters as much as it shows them to be ignorant. So we teach them.

A few years ago my last-period ninth graders possessed an unusual capacity for nastiness. Whenever possible, any of a dozen of them would feed on each other's rudeness, like gutted sharks in a feeding frenzy will engorge their own bowels. During a unit on the Holocaust, I was absent for a scheduled showing of "Genocide," a gruesome and disturbing episode from the *World at War* series. I desperately wanted to be present to monitor the showing but was simply too ill, and the film was rented for just that day. I felt most of my kids were sophisticated enough to behave in my absence—especially with so riveting a film—so I told my sub to show it.

All went well in my first four classes. Students were moved by the scenes and eager to learn more. But seeing a sub in my place only whetted the appetites of my last-hour "sharks."

During the showing of the film, eight or ten students talked and joked with each other and paid little attention except to mock some of the horrible scenes. My sub's attempts to quiet them were ignored. But she took names and described each person's behaviors specifically. The next day the class was silent at the beginning of the period, knowing I'd heard about the previous day and waiting for a lecture. I held the documentation in my hand.

After giving a reading assignment, I called the offenders one by one to my desk, showed them the notes, and asked if any of the observations were untrue. None denied what was written about them. I explained to each person that they would make up the hour they had wasted after school either that night or the next. Each was to make arrangements with his or her parents to stay after. The arrangements were to be made immediately.

—What?

—Yes. You can use the phone next door.

—What will I say?

—Whatever needs to be said, I guess.

Yes. While the class read, each of the offenders walked to a phone in the small office across the hall, called a parent, and explained that he or she would be staying late. If necessary they explained why, each in his or her own way.

I didn't wish to shame them, though I was still incensed by their blasphemous treatment of so serious a topic. I felt it especially important, then, for them to connect with their parents in a way that would encourage careful behavioral choices from here on.

After this, each child's behavior told me none of them wanted to repeat the experience of having to call home. They sensed an alliance between their parents and myself that would move quickly to repress revolting behavior. The class exited the year nicely.

GRADING

I hate grading. Unfortunately most everyone except teachers likes grades. Even commissioned studies of our schools insist on rating them A through F. The pass-fail system is used in some places, particularly in elementary schools where educators reasoned youngsters could then avoid early self-labeling as an A or C or F student. But in many of these schools parents are urging a return to the old system.

Sometimes students in upper grades who receive special help can be graded pass-fail in those classes where they are mainstreamed. But when I ask if they'd like to be graded pass-fail,

—Well what is this "pass"? Is it like a C or a D or what?
—It's not like that. A "pass" means you've met my expectations in this class, that you've done a satisfactory job.
—So what would that be?
—What do you mean?
—A "satisfactory"—would that be like a C then, or what?

Given a choice, students usually prefer even a D to a "pass." At least they think they know what a D means.

For now, it appears letter grades are too deeply entrenched in public school tradition to be dislodged. Indeed, grading is a phenomenon perpetuated throughout our culture from eggs to used cars, from meat to municipal credit ratings. But at least with meat and eggs, grade A is somewhat consistent in meaning.

THE EDUCATIONAL WAREHOUSE
A4 DISCOUNT DISTRIBUTORS, INC.
3 Perlman Drive, Spring Valley
N.Y. 10977   Tel: (914)426-ABCD

* ORIGINAL INVOICE * T1A19977
Z/C 10923
DATE: 04/20/95 SALES-REP: LI   PAGE: 1

ITEM-NUMBER   QTY UM PRICE   AMOUNT

    FE5192   1   EA   9.99   9.99
      POWER TEACHING

                  GROSS-AMT: 9.99
                                 .00

Grades in schools are more subjective, like a salesman's rating of used cars. It's certainly true that one teacher's A is another's B; moreover, the difficulty of a class is not considered in the grade.

We all know the inequities connected with grading and how sad it is when this is the only measure of a child's success in school. I hate grading, but I can't escape using grades. So I use them to strengthen my power base.

Awarding points for achievement—points I can later convert to grades—empowers me with great flexibility: I can do anything with points. I can reward a diligent child by inflating the total slightly when she falls just short of the grade I want for her. I can invite appropriate student involvement each day by awarding a point or withholding a point, depending.

With points, I can encourage more effort from kids by intentionally creating a low curve at mid-quarter—letting them think they're in danger of getting less than they're used to getting—if I want to. Sometimes a class needs that prodding. In rare instances I may take points away.

Mostly though, points are added, not deducted. For example, a large assignment is due Friday, but I wish to spread the paper-correcting over the entire week. If students have had several weeks to do this task, I may offer a point or two for papers turned in early. Similarly, I can deduct a point or two for late papers rather than insisting—hard-ass fashion—that all lates lose a whole grade, or that they take a zero.

That's another thing. Zeros. Kids soon learn they can average two equal assignments, an A and an F, for instance, into a C. But a 20 and a 0 average into a 10, which could convert to an F. Using points, students can less afford to ignore an assignment.

With tests and longer papers I give grades that convert to points, and vice versa. This allows me to reward any effort. On a 50-point test, 10 may be an F but not a 0: something is recorded in the grade book.

A lot of trouble? Perhaps. I do have to add things up eventually. But I've learned. For smaller assignments, I use a 4, 3, 2, 1, 0 system. For larger things I may multiply those points by 2, 3, 4, or 5. Too many points, and the point becomes meaningless. I don't want that. Here's one important reason.

On sheets of graph paper I list the students in each class. Every day I record in those squares attendance, tardiness, *and* a 1, .5, or 0 as a daily grade. A "1" indicates positive participation; ".5" means flagging attention or minimal effort; a "0" means no effort or that the student disturbed others.

If we have a class discussion, anyone who offers an honest insight earns an extra point. This rewards the thoughtful-vocal, who may not excel in other phases of the subject. Within days I have a visual record of a child's progress, which I can then use to urge a student toward more positive efforts. It works quickly when the student sees that daily participation can make up nearly 25 percent of the total grade.

"It's unfair," I was told by a parent, "to mark Jody off for her behavior." Jody was pretty, well-dressed, and very bright. She was also arrogant and rude to all but her one friend in my second-period class. Frequently she entertained herself and her snob friend by mimicking the responses of other kids or rolling her eyes back in her head when she judged an answer was stupid.

Occasionally she would snicker. I hate that. I hate haughtiness and snobbery in kids: I believe nothing is more mean-spirited, and in truth, such behavior is bigotry. When I first noticed this attitude, I asked her quietly why she would want to make others feel low. Smiling sweetly, she answered, "Oh, do I do that?" No admission, no denial, just contempt.

When she continued to mock and chide and belittle the others, I warned her I would lower her grade.

—You can't do that. You can't drop my grade just because you think I should be nicer to other kids. That's not fair.

—If life were fair, Jody, you'd have to share your brains and good looks with most of those kids. And they could share their tolerance for snobs with you.
—Hrummph!

For crimes against humanity, I lowered Jody's grade from an A to a B. It was a mistake—mean-spirited and vengeful—and both she and her parents were outraged. I relented, restored the A and vowed to find a way to incorporate behavior into my evaluation system. I felt justified; after all, in the real world, behavior often enhances or negates achievement. And parents have always supported the idea of giving credit for effort—on elementary school report cards my kids always received grades for attitude and effort. Besides, I had long wanted to establish daily incentives and also to reward kids for class discussion.

So for the second term I instituted the daily grade, defined as a single point given for positive or appropriate participation that aids learning. Distracting others would result in no point being awarded.

Jody and her friend remained smug, but rarely did either demean the efforts of others. They were outwardly civil and laughed with, and not at, their classmates. I knew their attitudes hadn't changed, but they were more accepting of others and less contemptuous in their verbal responses. Each of them needed that point because by the end of the quarter the daily points totaled 40 or more.

On some occasions I'll throw in a bonus point, for example, for the first person to volunteer doing her speech, or for that student who remembered to close the windows during the fire drill, or one each for the whole class for remaining silent and studious while I spoke to the principal outside my room. Or an extra point for letting me whisper the day I came in with laryngitis, or one for behaving well for the sub. And when a class has misbehaved, I can penalize each student a point—then offer them each the chance, if I choose, to earn it back the next day, double or nothing.

I hate grades, but I admit they are a powerful lever with most kids. And for me, points offer flexibility that straight letter grading does not. In effect, I give form and substance to those proverbial "brownie points." Best of all, I can do anything I like using points.

"Hey, You!"

"C'mon back and pick up that pop can. Hey! C'mon back here! Who is that kid? Any of you guys know that kid's name, the one who spilled soda all over your lockers here? You kids aren't even supposed to have pop in school. Now we've got a mess here." One of the great annoyances of teaching in the halls before school, after school, and during the passing of classes is confronting inappropriate behaviors of kids we don't know. We can't depend on the student's peers to give up the name, and we certainly can't expect a kid who doesn't know us to honor a request to return, especially if the school is a large one. A few things can help lessen our futility and at the same time reinforce our power base.

First, don't shy from doing hall duty. When I was a rookie in the junior high, I heard a colleague complaining about being assigned the duty of patrolling halls before school. John, a veteran phys-ed teacher, overheard and confronted the complainer, saying, "I do some of my best teaching in the halls."

I thought this a curious comment: I'd not considered my teaching role to extend beyond the classroom. But it's true: many opportunities for guiding the learning of kids, especially for teaching self-discipline and civic responsibilities are presented in the hall, and in other non-classroom environs.

We teach to the whole school and to *all* its kids. Locking ourselves in our space with the notion that we "specialize" is a cowardly and irresponsible pretext that shields us not just from duties we perceive as unpleasant, but from the respect of our peers as well. I watched John greet, praise, confront, and promote a climate of comfort in the areas he visited.

"Brad," he called to a ninth grader who just moments before had stooped near a locker, retrieving books scattered about the floor. "That's a good thing you did, helping that seventh grader collect those things before the other kids could kick them down the hall." John had seen the books spill in a mild collision of two anxious seventh graders, and the other boy, in a panic to reach his next class on time, had left the scene without offering to help fix the damage.

In his seventh-grade phys-ed class John would later find the boy who scurried off and explain how it's okay to stop and help, that any teacher in the hall will write a tardy excuse for that. "I'll get you a pass, Brad, in case you're late to your next class."

Kids eagerly eavesdrop when a teacher talks with a student. Any of them near now know that this particular teacher, John, will support responsible behavior. In a similar situation, and given a choice of doing the right thing or of scampering, some may sacrifice their anonymity and stay. Most kids like doing good, especially with a respected teacher's approval. A few witnesses to this scene may sometime emulate Brad's behavior.

In addition, John has a "supporter" for two more years in the seventh grader who was helped. Look on out-of-classroom supervision as part of the large scheme of teaching: we can do some of our best work there.

Second, learn names.

—Lenora, please come back and clean up the mess you've left here.
—How did you know my name? I don't have you for a teacher.
—I like to know everyone's name where I work. I appreciate your returning: you don't feel someone else should clean up after you, do you?

You say your memory is poor, you have 150 kids in five classes, and normally you can't call them by name before second semester. That's too bad: there is tremendous power in specificity, for we can't expect persons whose names we don't know to respect us. I study very hard the first day of school—very hard—so that I know most kids' names by the second day. I can't give better advice than that every teacher make this effort.

Many kids like to remain nameless for a variety of sad reasons. Some hope to cower in passivity, having found most recognition hurtful in the past. A few, like vandals, hope to leave dirty deeds to the knowledge only of their peers.

It's a huge ethical violation not to know who your charges are. It's also an invitation to vulnerability and is therefore stupid. (One reason substitute teachers have classroom management problems is that kids can act out and not be specifically confronted.) Who you don't know can hurt you. And who you don't know may also *be* hurting. Resolve to learn the names of each of your students by the second day. It's possible.

But what about the names of those wandering the halls? In many schools students near your room prior to first-hour class have lockers there, or friends with lockers. You will soon observe potential problem students acting in ways that border on mischievousness. Ask a colleague for the names, or ask a student you know or ask the students themselves *before* you have reason to confront them for negative behaviors. Just knowing you know them will encourage a measure of propriety.

Kids regard us positively for taking the trouble to know them, especially during those first days. They are often amazed that we learn so quickly, so easily (it seems) and often believe us to be brighter than we are—sometimes brighter than *they* are, even. Those first days are when we must build power if we are to have it. Being able to name people with as much confidence as we use the terms of the curriculum we teach is a talent that commands notice and respect.

We are not likely, however, to learn every child's name in an institution of a thousand kids. There will be times when "Hey, you!" is our best available response. Some kids will respond to that, especially if they know us by reputation. Then we have a chance to learn their names and to instruct them.

If they run off, however, and the hair bristles on the back of your neck, don't pursue them down stairwells, hollering "Stop, thief!" like a fat butcher wielding a machete after a dog with a dozen linked sausages. That will only force them to sprint through densely peopled halls while you, in hot pursuit, muss your looks and convulse your ire to where it must spill into your next class.

Don't look ridiculous here; appearances are important. Your manner and demeanor, your poise, are powerful tools in shaping how young kids regard you. Instead, note the time, the subject's appearance, and subtly inquire of kids you know as to whom this person might be. And don't be surprised if the same kid, curious about whether the "Hey, you!" was meant for him or wishing to test your powers of recall, should appear later in this same vicinity. That's okay: you'll be ready this time and far more effective (and generous too) than if you'd actually pursued and apprehended the youngster. Moreover, you might just catch him or her doing something good. In any case, be proud knowing you resisted the precipitous urge to "set things right, right now."

PART III

Testing the Limits of Your Power

RIGHT AND REASONABLE

Throughout this book I've spoken of rightness and reasonableness as the principles for guiding how we shape our teaching environment. I've suggested that even without specific definitions, students and teachers probably agree about 99 percent of the time on what things are right and what are reasonable. Of course, agreeing sometimes takes time and discussion and, especially, an ability to stand back from a situation. But generally, kids know, and we know, when we or they have been right and when we've been reasonable. Unfortunately, I can't suggest that teaching according to these concepts would be supported by your state statutes, by federal law, or by your school district's policies. But regardless of laws or policies, I wish to be more definitive about these concepts. I feel this is necessary because in the following chapters I'll be talking about truly difficult students—those who may be in the 1 percent who cannot be expected to understand what is right and reasonable. When dealing with these students, it is important that you understand these principles clearly, for many of these students have amazing manipulative powers, astute intellects, and a tenacious indignation and self-righteousness that can press you to doubt yourself.

My teaching philosophy holds that the following principles—but not these exclusively—are right. With the exception of that 1 percent, I hold that students too perceive these principles as right. Moreover, if ever a school policy or state statute were to appear to oppose these rights, I am confident the public would overwhelmingly support our insistence that these rights be respected.

1. It is right that personalities not be violated.
2. It is right that persons in our workplaces recognize, respect, and support our entitlement to basic human dignity insofar as we respect the same entitlement for them.
3. It is right that we not be obstructed physically, emotionally, or intellectually in pursuit of doing our jobs.

Because we teach, it is incumbent upon us to forbid that anyone defile, denigrate, insult, curse, or otherwise violate who we are, or obstruct what we've been commissioned to do. Because we teach, we must confront—sometimes with righteous indignation—attempts to violate us physically, emotionally, and intellectually. Because we teach young people—children, who need to know acceptable ways of challenging similar indignities—we must not allow ourselves to ignore affronts. If we do, particularly in our classrooms, we have failed our students and ourselves.

Many of us have seen these things pass without comment:

• A student sits with his back to the teacher as the lesson is explained.
• A student swears at a teacher or fellow student, with little or no provocation.
• A student defies directions and correction and so obstructs the teacher's ability to provide learning, maintain order, or assure a safe environment for other students.

I remember a colleague telling of a student he'd referred to the office seven times for fighting. Each time the boy returned from administrative intervention remorseless and angry and ready to spill more havoc in this co-ed phys-ed class of 40 seventh graders. Soon another fight would ensue. The teacher complained,

—What can I do? They keep sending him back!
—Refuse to take him back.
—I can't do that.

Baloney. He *must* do that. It's wrong to allow one disturbed youngster to perpetuate a reign of terror.

Teachers must first be *confident* of the right to dignified treatment for ourselves and all those in our charge. Then we must act, for kids despise indecision, threats, wimpiness, and tears. Offenses must be confronted without shouting or fanfare, though the best time may not be immediately. If the attention may confer positive peer regard on the offender, or if it could trigger a violent reaction, it's better to make an appointment: "We'll talk after class, John." Physical threats and fighting are exceptions, of course.

It's reasonable to wait until the end of a class period to specifically address, for instance, an incident of verbal impropriety—insult, swearing, or sexual innuendoes—behaviors that if confronted before a group sometimes make us appear clownish (or embarrass the victim). Simply addressing the perpetrator with "Richard, we'll talk a minute after class" tells others you've taken action. And if you have a message for other kids, the offender will pass it along later when they ask, "What'd he say?"

When we operate confidently in our resolve to insist on what's right, students sense that and often decide not to test us. They know that our teaching philosophy—which encourages them to make good choices—will also protect them from poor choices made by others. They feel empowered to choose well, urged by our powerful expectations of them.

I believe we must trust the public to support us in insisting our relationships with colleagues, administrators, children, agencies, and parents be predicated on mutual respect. What we do in orchestrating such relationships I'll loosely define as reasonable.

When I've been reasonable and applied strategies to urge reasonable change, it's rare that I must exclude a child permanently from my class. Some kids, however, are sick and need specialized treatment. We must be prepared then to insist on other placement for them, because it is reasonable to arrange that the rights of many be protected from the whims or illnesses of a few. (I'm not supporting majority rule; indeed, nowhere do I intend to suggest that our classrooms follow the democratic model. That is usually disastrous. If I were to advocate anything, it would be the benevolent dictatorship.)

The minority viewpoint often strengthens our classrooms. We encourage free exchange of thought. It's exciting. But we must be less encouraging of free expression of behavior. Of course "appropriate" is necessarily ambiguous, for it allows people flexibility and creativity in choosing behaviors that fit how they see a situation. These choices may sometimes be distracting but do not measurably obstruct the learning process. Students who are defiant toward us or their classmates, however, must assume immediate self-control when confronted or be excluded posthaste. They may be "good" kids having a bad day, and later they can explain. But for the good of other students and for shoring up or preserving our assigned authority, these kids must be immediately out of our presence.

In such cases, a "reasonable" removal does not mean exclusion after months of hoping for change, or until the child can be tested, or until contact has been made with parent, guardian, social worker, or parole officer. No. "Reasonable" means right now. Ask the person to leave and give them a place to go: the principal's office, counseling office, hallway, vacant nearby room, or any other place that is safe to them and that they can reasonably be expected to find (I will know by the first day of school the options available to me during each teaching period—see "Know Your Turf," pages 36–39).

Notify the office via room phone or student messenger where the student can be found, and proceed with your lesson. It's probably not convenient then to fill out a lengthy form that the student would anyway rather destroy than present to someone for the purpose of self-incrimination. It's unreasonable to expect a teacher to take time from the class to detail reasons for referral. A written pass with a single word—"insubordinate"—should suffice.

If the student refuses to leave, contact the administration for help via phone or student messenger. If you can't make contact that way, do not panic. Say something like: "Of course, stay if you insist, if this is where you want to be. I'm not going to quarrel with you."

Afterward, put the entire incident to an administrator in writing. Insist that the child be dealt with before you admit him or her the next day. Ask for a written explanation from the administrator of how the student was handled—or not handled. That is reasonable.

To be right, we must have documentation. Get support from students—from anyone who was present and can testify to the specifics of your actions. Ask them to write down all they saw and heard, and have them date and sign their statements.

We may exclude a student who threatens us or others in our charge. And I do not interpret this narrowly as meaning physical threats only. A threat needn't be sticks and stones—it rarely is, in fact—to hurt, humiliate, and destroy.

Teachers are not jailers or prison guards. Nor are we whipping posts or receptacles for the emotional garbage each of the 150-plus students whom we see each day may bring with them. Because we teach, some garbage will be left with us. That's to be expected. But we needn't accept being showered with it.

We are reasonable when we confront nuisance behaviors and defiant acting-out in ways that convey neither malice nor apology. Explosive situations are like grease fires, and they are best controlled by anticipating them. It's supremely important that we map strategies for a wide range of behaviors so that we can take positive, confident action when necessary—poise is usually a companion to preparedness. Blandly tolerating insolence lowers kids' esteem for us and makes our chances of connecting positively with them even less likely. After all, they know what's right.

In summary, "right" consists of our entitlement—and that of our students—to dignified treatment in the progress of our jobs. It assumes a high correlation—99 percent or so—between what we understand dignified treatment to be and what adolescents understand it to be. "Reasonable" means that we've offered students numerous chances, and that to protect our entitlements—including our right to teach and students' rights to learn—we've suggested ways of correcting threatening behaviors. Dignity commands power. We empower others and ourselves by insisting on dignified treatment.

THE POWER OF DOCUMENTATION

Nothing serves the issue of "right" like notes specifying behaviors, attitudes, and especially conversations with kids who serve early notice that they intend to pick away at your power base. In most cases, teachers can see or sense a potential problem. A beginning step is to specify the observed behavior, date the note, and confront the person with your observation. Ask the individual to sign the note. Often he or she will. And often this message discourages further acting out. In the most difficult cases, however, you are building support for the ultimate, necessary removal of the offending person.

Documentation that is written and signed by the student can be a singularly powerful tool in modifying behavior and in supporting your position with parents, counselors, and administrators.

I had spoken with Julie on three occasions about excessive talking, leaving her seat, and about acting to gain the attention of several boys in the classroom. When Julie's Tuesday was a copy of an unproductive Monday, I kept her after class and asked her to explain why I was displeased with her. She pretended not to know.

—Fine. Let's just stay together until you can come up with a reasonable guess. Thirty minutes tonight, thirty tomorrow, thirty every night until you arrive at some notion of why I am displeased.
—Well, what if I tell you why?
—No. Write it down.
—Then what?

—Then you can go.

—I can? (She grabs some paper and begins writing.)

Tuesday, Sept. _____

I think Mr. M. may be displeased with me because I was not listening to his directions. First off, I was late to class because I was talking to Troy, and then when I came in I talked to Marty while Mr. M. was talking, and then I sat down and got right up to sharpen my pencil and I talked to Steve and Randy on the way, and when I sat down Mr. M. said I was not to leave my seat or speak without permission but I did that a few more times anyway. He said kinda the same stuff to me yesterday. He said I'm distracting others. I'm not doing so good in here because I know lots of these guys and I like to talk more than listen. I also threw some stuff, bits of erasers at Mary, and blew my nose real loud once when I didn't have to.

—Is this enough?

—Yes.

—Can I go now?

—Sure. Just sign your name there at the bottom.

—Okay. Now I can go.

—Sure.

—Wait. (Pointing) You're not going to show that to my dad or anything like that, are you? I'm not kidding— he'll kill me. He'll ground me for months. Please don't show that to him.

—He'd be upset?

—Yes!

—How interesting . . .

I made copies of Julie's note and kept one handy; I could produce it any time she began to revert to her old inappropriate behaviors. She caused few problems the rest of the term.

"Wait a minute," you say. "Foul!" "Dirty pool!" "Entrapment!" The man is manipulative, insidious, unscrupulous, base, and vile: he's exploited the poor child's yearning to leave school. She'd do almost anything to join her friends before they all scatter for home. What next, blackmail? "It's disgusting, his holding that incrimination like a knife to her throat."

Yes, perhaps, but if it enables her to stop salivating over Marty, Steve, and Randy to the distraction of the whole class, I can bear the guilt.

If your sentiments are with the child here, save them for yourself. When you have Julie, you'll understand. Be careful, though, for with Julie, gentler treatment is no favor to her. We rarely help kids by using less guile in correcting them than they use in creating opportunities for correction. Furthermore, students would often rather incriminate themselves this way than have the incident leave the room.

I like this technique because it keeps third-party involvement available but at a negotiable distance. And, ironically, it has many times forged positive bonds between the student and myself. The child appreciates my attention and also my refusal to cop out by simply sending him or her to the office or phoning home. Yes, I'm extorting appropriate behaviors, but the child knows how I might have made much larger trouble.

Few students require the heavier strategies I present next in this manual; softer approaches will correct student behaviors 99 percent of the time—but only if students understand your attitudes and are certain of your resolve.

CRAZY FOR POWER

My worst fear is that some morning I'll wake up and hate the idea of going into the classroom, that I'll no longer want to work with kids. I rarely think about feeling that way, but occasionally I'm asked what frightens me most about my work. I think then how horrible it would be to be angry or always fearful or desperate in my job—and then inevitably I think of Lenny.

Unofficially, Lenny was crazy. Most everyone at our junior high knew Lenny's insanity far exceeded what was normal for junior high kids, but nevertheless, he was one of 29 students in my last-hour English class. I was younger then and so assumed Lenny was a permanent part of the job. After all, anyone can handle the "good" kids. Right? At the time I thought I wasn't a teacher if I couldn't handle the likes of Lenny.

Fortunately, a colleague who remembered Lenny from the previous year suggested I document his behavior "in case he kills someone or something." He was only half serious, I think. But I took the advice, and what follows are several examples of my documentations and, perhaps most importantly, the scenario I believe inspired my present notions about the importance of power in teaching.

—August 28. Talked with Lenny _____ today about his behavior. He'd muttered complaints, sworn, and scratched loudly on his paper until it ripped, all during a silent writing period. Later he provoked three other students by taking their materials. He periodically disturbed others by pushing his papers on the floor and by emitting frequent whistling noises.

A version of this chapter appeared as an article in the March issue of *Learning89* (Vol. 17, No. 7).

I'd been pleased with him the past few days and said so, but admitted then that he'd upset me today. This brought a gleam to his blue eye, while he stared dead on with his brown eye. I explained how limited I was for time to see each of the kids and asked that he take care of himself—bring his own materials, avoid disturbing others, etc.—and he agreed to help me out.

Lenny interpreted my early concern for him as weakness, to be exploited for his satisfaction. Since attacking wimps met some of Lenny's power needs, the problem at this point was indeed mine—and sure to become even more acute.

—September 4. Lenny arrived on time today, but without pencil and paper. He then took Alan's. When I confronted him, he shouted, "You didn't tell us!" then grumbled, "I hate Mr. Mahle." A few minutes later he fell backward in his chair, crashing to the floor, then kicked and thrashed noisily in attempting to get up. The rest of the class and I ignored him as best we could.

Through his counselor, I was aware of the history of abuse in Lenny's family. I naively assumed that this entitled him to special consideration even at the expense of other students. I also learned he was incorrigible in every class, yet was rarely referred to the office. If his other teachers could tolerate him, why not I? Lenny was always threatening to run away. I hoped he would—how sad is that?—so I could save face by "handling the problem myself," by not getting the office involved.

—October 22. After nearly a week absent, Lenny was back today. Almost immediately I asked him to leave after he referred to another student several times as a "faggot," then said to a boy near him, "Joe, Jane (a girl two seats away) wants your c – – k." Muttering profanities, Lenny left for the assistant principal's office.

The office had little impact on Lenny. He saw nothing to lose by behaving as he did. Lenny had discovered the immense power in being crazy: though physically unimpressive, everyone in my class was terrified of him. I learned from that. When once more he returned from the vice-principal's office remorseless and unchanged, I decided to act a little crazy myself.

October 22
Dear (Assistant Principal),
I thought you'd want to know that Lenny _____ will not be allowed back into my class tomorrow. Today was his last chance to correct himself under my supervision.

After returning from the office, he continued to act out by cursing his change in seating. Then he leaned back and put his dirty stockinged feet up on his desk. He talked out frequently during the remaining time and left his seat on at least four occasions without permission. Near the end of the period I came to Lenny and said, "Lenny, you know we are all hoping for the best for you, but you are making this difficult." Lenny responded, "Don't talk to me!"

I don't intend to talk to Lenny anymore. I thought you would like to know, so you can prepare for him when he appears on your doorstep at the beginning of last period tomorrow. Lenny's disruptions have significantly impaired the the ability of his classmates to learn. I will not be able to readmit him until he has made significant, positive changes in his behavior.
Sincerely,
B.

I delivered this letter at the end of the day, and left feeling great. At last I'd done something. For the good of the class, I was refusing to let Lenny return. That seemed right. That was right! How could I doubt it. He had cost us countless hours of learning. Yes, absolutely, I was certainly right in this.

Next morning, this was in my mailbox:

October 22
Mr. M.,
Please see me regarding Lenny _____.

It was signed by the assistant principal. Later . . .

—You wished to see me about Lenny.
—I can't have him here—well maybe for today, but he can't spend his English period every day on my doorstep.

—He can't be in my class.

—Well, would you have his schedule changed? Do you think Ms. _____ would do a better job with him?

—No.

—Then you would just be giving your problem to her?

—No.

—How so?

—I'm giving him to you.

—(Smiling, suggesting "surely you jest.") He can't stay here. You know that. Lenny has to be in class.

—Not mine.

—Well, should he be placed in the Behavior Management class?

—I don't care. I referred him weeks ago for that. What happened?

—We could never get hold of his mother to get permission for testing.

—I see.

—We can't just put him in that class without having given him the tests and without getting parent permission.

—I see.

—We'll try to get permission again. In the meantime, you'll have to do your best with him.

—No. I won't take him back.

—You are saying you refuse to take him?

—Are you saying I have to take him?

—Well . . .

—(Interrupting) Suppose this: Suppose you order me to have Lenny in my class. And suppose I summarize the pages of documentation I've shared with you and send them home in a letter to the parents of each child in that class. Suppose I explain how I've turned over the problem of Lenny to you for remediation, but that you have said I must keep the boy in class. Suppose I apologize for the inconvenience this may cause their child, but that all questions should be directed to you.

What do you think you will hear from these parents?

—Suppose I cite you for insubordination?

—Parents are entitled to know what is going on around their kids. The letter I mentioned seems reasonable.

—You would do that?

—I will not have Lenny in my class unless you order it. He will be on your doorstep tomorrow, and I will never see him again, unless I hear from you. . . .

Later that day . . .

Dear Mr. M.,
We were able to place Lenny in the Behavior Management program on an emergency basis until such time as all the testing can be completed.
Sincerely,
A.P.

Lenny was never in my room again. With him went a number of things: the whistling and drowning-turkey noises, the spectacular crash landings, the muttered obscenities—and suddenly an end to the crude additions penned on the anatomies of the athletes in my classroom editions of *Sports Illustrated.*

Other things were discovered: the exhilaration of teaching without distraction, noticeable relief in students who'd been harassed and threatened by Lenny, and major increases in the quantity and quality of students' work.

Mostly though, the experience with Lenny showed me how to acquire legitimate power. First, by being right: removing Lenny was unquestionably correct (the greatest error was in keeping him so long), because he was stealing learning from others in my classroom. Secondly, it's reasonable for parents to know what the school environment is like for their children. When I offered to acquaint the parents of Lenny's classmates with documented facts, I had the leverage with the administration to insist on what I knew was right. I have insisted ever since.

An experience begun as a crisis evolved into an opportunity from which I learned that I could establish a legitimate power base in my classroom, predicated on common notions of "right" and "reasonable."

I had tried encouraging this boy, reinforcing positive behaviors, and one-to-one tutoring. I was never sarcastic or malicious in correcting him. His classmates found my patience with him trying: "Can't you get him out of here?" I guess I'd thought, "No. He has as much right to be here as any of you." Yet I'd referred him the second day for special services and testing. In the end, he had not cooperated, his mother was unreachable, and the administration was too busy. Until I insisted.

Before Lenny was sent away for long-term psychiatric care, he continued to upset classes. His placement in the Behavior Management program proved valuable for my students and helped me regain my enthusiasm for teaching. But for weeks after I excluded him, other teachers let him perpetuate vulgar and menacing disruptions and block learning. Why? "I don't feel right giving my problem to someone else." "I've sent him to the office seven times, three times for fighting just this week. They just send him back."

Each day I'd looked forward to the absence list, hoping Lenny's name would appear there. With that as my prevailing hope, I hated teaching. Now I wonder how many others suffer that way. I wonder how long their students will be denied a comfortable learning space. And I wonder how many more Lennys will lose time getting the help they need while school personnel sheepishly resist doing what they know is right.

THE SACRIFICIAL GOAT

"You know, Jason was gone today, and we had the best class—even Chris and Larry did their work. And Andrea, you know she has such a case on Jason—every move he makes, she has to giggle. She was totally different—finished her work, even wrote some clever thoughts about what the year 2010 will be like. I didn't know she could be clever. When Jason is here, it seems I've got four or five problem kids. . . . It's terrible to say, but I hope he stays sick a long time. I mean, I look forward to the absence list just to see if his name is on it."

Any classroom has children whose behaviors are potentially disruptive. Most of these problems can be avoided by judiciously establishing a power base through knowing one's turf, being reasonably assertive, and empowering kids to take care of themselves. Other techniques for guiding them and encouraging positive behaviors are a large part of this manual. Occasionally though, a student appears who is not influenced by these strategies and who, unlike poor Lenny, is insidious in his or her design for your classroom and hopes to destroy it by enlisting the help of others. This person's main reason for being in school is to take pleasure in the disruptions he or she can provoke.

Phil was such a person. He thrived on peer attention and had the ability to incite others to behave badly—or well, if he so chose. Unfortunately, that was rarely his choice.

I inherited Phil from another teacher, who was worn with the demands of handling him. Phil was popular with a number of kids in my class. Phil was good-looking, "hip," very clever, and antagonistic toward all authority. I later learned he was also a hot source for drugs at our school. This eighth grader also boasted openly of his heavy partying.

Phil's words were eagerly awaited by the boys who admired him; they thought him clever at baffling teachers with sexual innuendoes and "druggie" talk. Indeed, Phil exuded an aura of expectancy—kids knew that things would happen in his presence. This made him appealing to many.

Other kids were afraid of Phil. He roamed with bigger, less-bright boys who would bully others at his goading. He also had a caustic, cruel wit and could neatly incise the self-esteem of peers by alluding to their stupidity, ugliness, awkwardness, or—at his nastiest—their slow development of male (or female) physical characteristics. Phil was vile. Period.

To his credit, however, Phil was bright about knowing the limits. He would push teachers just so far. For one thing, he wanted passing grades: his image demanded that others think him smart. And he thought enough of the institution to urge testimony of his intelligence from it.

For quite some time he was good in my class. I documented, however, all incidents where he muttered insults or sexual innuendoes, or spoke casually of partying or drugs. Nothing Phil did was without design—for peer approval, to test my indulgence, to exhibit his intelligence and knowledge of the world.

I soon learned his techniques: second-guessing information in order to draw attention to himself and thus make opportunity for delivery of innuendoes or outrageous opinions and conclusions. Other times he'd feign ignorance in hopes of provoking digressive discussion.

Still, many of the kids enjoyed me, and my class, more than they liked Phil. Within a few weeks he began to regard me with some disdain, for I'd been eroding his influence with many of his peers. Ultimately, my growing popularity with his friends irritated him to the point of a showdown.

One day he was evoking titters from several around him, and I found the source was his journal, which apparently contained some hot sexual content. Knowing how quickly he could incite others, my solution to ending the distraction was to confiscate the journal. Phil refused to turn this writing over to me:

—This is my property.
—Yes, but you're distracting others with it. I'll take it until the end of the hour.
—Like hell you will.
—Fine. Keep it. Put it aside. We'll talk later. For now, put the trash aside.
—Who says it's trash? You haven't read it.
—We'll talk later.

I had erred with Phil in first insisting he turn over the journal. He had goaded me into a power face-off, and my mistake in pressing to take the journal had allowed him the righteous declaration, "like hell you will." Luckily, I laid off: he would have fought me to the death for "his property." That was his sense of right, and many students would have sided with him.

I was wrong too in judging the material as "trash," and told him so later. But that conversation was Phil's undoing. When I apologized for attempting to seize the notebook and also for calling it "trash," he sensed an advantage. He became flip in a way I'd seen him work before. On those occasions he would either answer a question with a question, or he'd repeat what you said.

The first technique enabled him to pressure the questioner. The other, delivered in a mocking tone, discounted what you said. I probed to find out why he had begun the distraction.

—Why do you want to know?
I resisted answering. Instead I ventured boldly,
—Is it because you are a burnout and you have no control?
—Yeah, that's it. I'm a burnout and I have no control.
—Why do you come to school if you have no control?
No response.

—Is it because you like to hassle teachers?

—Yeah, it's because I like to hassle teachers.

—You come to school expressly for the purpose of disrupting classes and hassling teachers.

—I come to school to disrupt classes and to hassle teachers.

I documented this exchange, gave it to the principal, and refused to have Phil back, because I knew our school district policies allowed that students who come to school expressly for the purpose of misbehaving or getting others to misbehave can be excluded.

Phil was misplaced in my class, misplaced in the public school setting. He was ill, and a criminal preying on children. Ultimately he self-destructed in other classes too and was sent away for chemical-dependency treatment.

I don't know what became of him. It still worries me that he perhaps hasn't changed and is now an adult preying on children. Did I treat him too tenderly? I think not, for I never allowed him to incite others in the class to behave badly. But I had the advantage of knowing that when Phil was transferred to my class, he was leaving a class where he'd had just that effect.

In truth, even before he began acting out, I was prepared to sacrifice Phil if he was provoking negative behavior. I call this strategy "The Sacrificial Goat," and I have since used it in cases less extreme than his. Like any other ploy, it requires the "rightness" of documentation and the "reasonableness" of having tried the earlier interventions. Once it's clear these won't work and the classroom environment is worsening with the talent this person has for drawing in others, he or she must be removed. Permanently. "I'm sorry, Phil. You'll have to find another English class."

Before I make this pronouncement, I must have made arrangements, through the cooperation of counselors or administrators, for the person's placement. For instance, I will have agreed with them on an option for locating him elsewhere. With reasonable people, that is usually what happens, because most counselors and administrators are as eager as we are to provide proper placement for students.

But make no mistake: a student whose sole aim is to disrupt learning in your classroom can—and must!—go elsewhere. In fact, it is incumbent upon the teacher to initiate that happening. Do not allow yourself to feel you are giving your problem to someone else. This student is misplaced in your class and may well belong in a hospital.

Since I teach several sections of the same subject, similar problems are sometimes resolved with relative ease. Often, for instance, the child is not so much sinister as immature and can't learn in the presence of a "best" friend. I've then arranged to transfer one of them to another of my sections. This is most often the case: friends simply unable to be good together.

Or another teacher may take one of these people—as I took Phil in the earlier example. In any event, we must free ourselves of the miracle-worker myth—the belief that we must succeed with every child (or persevere like Anne Sullivan) or consider ourselves failures.

No individual can be allowed to routinely impede the learning of others. Intervene, document, call home, encourage, and cajole—give kids their chances—then put the problem where it belongs: with your administration.

If you have several bad actors, sacrifice the leader; the others will fall in line, often relieved to be back on track with you. More than once I've been uneasy in a parent conference when Mom or Dad, after announcing elation at the improvement in their youngster, follow with "I guess all he needed was to get away from _____." Why did I hesitate to make that happen?

Hoping a kid moves, runs away, or stays sick as an answer to a problem is totally wimpy. Teachers must empower themselves to act, and be deaf to suggestions that they are saddling others with their problems. That exploitive prattle has gained many proud teachers sleepless nights or early resignation. Ignore it. Document, make plans, then do what is reasonable and right. Ensuring a learning climate for your classroom may mean making a sacrifice. That's okay.

"Yeah, but I'll Get Sued."

Lenny and Phil are the exceptions, but either one of them might have ended my career. I had to accept the truth, not taught in teacher education classes, that we as individual teachers cannot save all kids. That doesn't mean kids can't be saved—only that no single one of us can save each and every one of them. Once I realized this limitation and accepted it, I began asking, "What next? Clearly I can't teach with stressors like Lenny and Phil." The answer of course is in knowing that other professionals and institutions exist for handling those kinds of kids.

But others must first be made acquainted with the need and, as was the case of my first administrator, they must sometimes be pressed to see the problem is not reasonably yours to resolve. Teachers who are too proud to admit they can't handle a situation slip inexorably toward mental breakdown and risk their families as well as their jobs. Teachers too timid to enlist help or to stand their professional ground will also fail. Representatives of both types counter my invocation with "Yeah, sure, but I'll get sued."

Perhaps—and I sympathize. I know how nervous we can be about legal liability. Chances for being sued seem far greater, however, when one fails to confront inappropriate behavior or confronts it without the certain resolve that if things get bad enough, I'll rightfully bid good-bye to this student.

A teacher who fails or refuses to make peace with throwing the final trump card often ends up verbally and emotionally abused by difficult students, and frequently discounted by the rest. That teacher's failure to confront defiance and demand dignity projects an image of terrible powerlessness and vulnerability that invites disdain from *all* students.

Remember: Students know what is reasonable and right and will respect you—not sue you—for acting in the best interests of the majority.

Still, it's wise to know the state statutes that spell out rights of students. Most teachers do not know them, and benignly assume every student is entitled to an education no matter how disruptive he or she is. Given the presence of bona fide criminals in some of our schools, one might conclude that this is largely true. These students are not entitled to an education in *your* classroom, however, if you have been reasonable in dealing with them and have adequately documented your attempts at remediating both their academic and behavioral problems.

Many alternatives are available, from placement in behavioral modification classes to homebound tutoring. Know the statutes and the alternatives. Look carefully at the following excerpt from Minnesota Statutes, Section 127.29, pertaining to grounds for dismissal. Sub division 1 reads:

No school shall dismiss any pupil without attempting to provide alternative programs of education prior to dismissal proceedings, except where it appears that the pupil will create an immediate and substantial danger to himself or to persons or property around him. Such programs may include special tutoring, modification of the curriculum for the pupil, placement in a special class or assistance from other agencies.

Have you tried providing an alternative program that might meet the recalcitrant person's educational needs? Yes. You've no doubt invited the person to meet after school with you. No doubt you've offered extra help with subject matter and have contacted parents or guardians with suggestions for help at home. You've encouraged, counseled, humored, cautioned, confronted. But nothing has deterred the person's aim of rendering you and your classroom dysfunctional.

Moreover, the student hates school and projects that to you in ways that threaten your authority and undercut your ability to teach others. Other placement is in order. Insist that it happen. Besides, being dismissed from your classroom is not tantamount to being dismissed from the school. This child has other chances: other sections to be placed in, other programs—alternatives that must be provided away from your room. Even after the person is gone, you'll have challenge enough regaining the learning that was lost while you offered all those second chances. Above all, don't feel guilty.

Subdivision 2 reads:

A pupil may be dismissed on the following grounds:
a. Willful violation of any reasonable school board regulation. Such regulation must be clear and definite to provide notice to pupils that they must conform their conduct to its requirements;
b. Willful conduct which materially and substantially disrupts the rights of others to an education;
c. Willful conduct which endangers the pupil or other pupils, or the property of the school.

If your state statutes read anything like this, I advise that you become well acquainted with school board regulations regarding pupil conduct. Also, in the above statute, much is subject to interpretation. Who is to interpret? Your students? No. Clearly you must decide if behaviors "materially and substantially" disrupt the rights of others to an education.

Perhaps as a guideline here you can consider how narrowly you would define "materially and substantially" if your own son or daughter were a student in your class. How long would you have your daughter sitting next to Phil? We must teach as though this were the case. Otherwise, you don't want me teaching your kids, even if your kid (and this is sometimes the case) is Lenny or Phil. (See "My Kid's in There Too!" pages 96–97.)

I think legislatures and school districts need to broaden the scope of these statutes and give more flexibility to teachers. Yet some teachers, out of ignorance or pride, fail to act even within their scope.

Perhaps it's sad that these statutes are not tested, that we aren't more often sued, and that testimony is not read into court records that would show the injustices done to students whose teachers act tentatively, or not at all, in protecting the rights of the many.

No. We'll not likely be sued for doing the right things. But if one of us is, we might be glad for the chance to discover interpretation of these statutes in court. Each of us might work then to combine the power of parents and teachers, and together to insist that adjudicators and legislatures recognize more definitively the rights of the majority of kids. Why, for instance, aren't they entitled to individual assessments and to programs geared to their uniqueness? A digression, perhaps, but not a question to be ignored if and when teachers are sued for excluding disruptive students while attempting to afford others at least a fraction of their educational entitlement.

"My Kid's in There Too!"

Lawsuits are rare, yet we fear removing kids like Lenny will invite lawsuits. But I've just found out about the Lenny in your class from guess who? That's right—my own kid is in there with him. The stuff I'm hearing about Lenny! It's time I checked it out. Good grief, if half what I've heard is true, my daughter can't be learning much—except that one crazy kid can intimidate a whole class and the teacher, too. She doesn't speak very well of you. "Why doesn't Mr. Simon just kick him out?" she asks.

I don't know exactly, but it doesn't seem right. The more I think of it, the more angry I become. That kid sounds awful, nasty, mean. Maybe I should check with the parents of the other 30 kids. Perhaps we should consider a class-action suit and insist our kids get an equal opportunity to learn? Clearly the kids in other classes are getting a fairer shake. How about that? As if having Lenny wasn't stress enough.

It throws a different light there, to at least consider how you'd deal with problem kids if your child was in your class with them. Parents want the best for their kids. If you'd change your classroom approach to take care of your own, you'd better decide that it's right to do it for other parents. Resolve to do right for kids knowing that parents will support you. After all, don't you hope your child's teachers will find the energy you have—the energy and resolve to dispense with handwringing, whining, and the poor-me, wimpy posturing that has curdled teachers' self-esteems, eroded their effectiveness, and made them want to quit? We hope so.

Now, take ten minutes to list things you know are right and reasonable, that you can choreograph into class management and lesson delivery, and resolve to improve your teaching effectiveness (as well as your liability against court action) by enhancing your power base with some of these. Consider not just items of discipline, but all areas of your teaching from the appearance of your room and the nature and quantity of homework (and when it's assigned) to the amount of time you expect kids to listen to a lecture. List below whatever you'd change or add to enrich your own child's learning and enjoyment of this class.

_____

_____

_____

_____

_____

_____

_____

_____

_____

_____

_____

Enlisting Parent Power for Positive Change

I've written of two kinds of parental power. The first is direct support of teachers, characterized by hands-on, cooperative planning and by discussion and encouragement relative to motivating a youngster toward positive change. This cooperation is often sparked by a teacher's benevolent interest in a child, which when tactfully expressed to parents, helps forge an alliance for change. It is not a result of "tattling."

The second kind of parent power is theoretical support. This differs from direct support in one important respect: theoretical support plays only in a child's mind, where he or she imagines vivid parental backing for the teacher's position.

Children base this vision on their belief that parents and teachers share common understandings of what is right and reasonable. When they picture this alliance and the forces that might be brought to bear on them from both home and school, what they imagine is usually far more persuasive than the real pressures could be. Subsequently, kids empower themselves to change, and we all win.

A third type of parent support is philosophical support, or support for common-sense educational issues dear to our hearts, like the value of smaller class sizes, the need to restructure funding for education, and the immediate need to free teachers of responsibility for teaching defiant and disruptive youngsters in the mainstream.

Many teachers believe only parents who are also teachers support these issues. Such thinking is narrow and presumptuous and deeply undermines parental and public approval for our causes. These same teachers bemoan lack of parental backing but rarely contact parents without whining and handwringing, creating a tone that suggests powerlessness. Some refuse to contact parents at all.

We are too often careful not to arouse parents. Yet certainly more would support us philosophically *and* directly if only they knew the truth. Parents who'd prove valuable allies have no time for whining, handwringing, or sifting the truth from the bull. Still teachers and administrators often seem loath to tell all.

> —Drugs? Oh, drugs are no more a problem at Jefferson than they are at any other junior high. (I see your kid hanging with some of the burnouts—is that why you ask?)
>
> —Oh, the food fight. Just a few kids got out of hand. You heard what? Well, you know how kids will exaggerate. (The ketchup stains on your daughter's $40 outfit were not exaggerated, eh?)
>
> —Lenny? So you've heard about him. Quite a character all right, but I think we're making progress with him. Most of the kids just ignore him. (It's tough though for your daughter to concentrate when he crashes to the floor next to her, looks up her dress, and makes animal noises.)

I recall a conference with the mother of a particularly bright student. She asked if her child was being challenged in my class.

> —Well, Gary's writing encompasses the breadth and the depth of my questions. He'll have to challenge himself with more difficult authors on the subject.
>
> —What do you mean, "challenge himself"?
>
> —I mean Gary can have time to go to the library—I can suggest some books—and he can probe as deeply as he wishes. He's left his classmates behind, I'm afraid.
>
> —Haven't you any more than that for him?

—I would need to design a course exclusively for him. I haven't time to do that. I have to teach language arts to 150 students besides Gary. As it is, the paper load is overwhelming. I simply haven't time to do more.
—That's terrible. You admit then that my son is not realizing his learning potential here.
—Yes. I admit it. And I'm sorry.
—Sorry? What good does that do? You're the teacher!
—Doesn't seem fair, does it.
—I should say not—and it's so frustrating. What would you do if you were me?
—If I were you, I'd find everyone in this district who thought like I did and instigate a class-action suit demanding equal opportunity—a chance to realize full academic potential—for these kids.

When my supervisor heard I'd had a conference with this woman, he asked for a summary. I explained it as you've read here. His mouth dropped when I mentioned "suit."

—You recommended she do what?
—Sue the district.
—You actually suggested that?
—Yes.
—Why would you say that?
—I felt she was right.
—(Pause) You felt she was right?
—Yes. Do I sense some, ah, disapproval?
—I think you might have exercised more, ah, discretion.

Discretion. The better part of valor, someone wrote. Four years later I was on a committee to develop a high-potential program for junior high English students. Gary's mother was also on the committee.

Someone had done as I'd advised. Parents had haunted the administrator's offices until action was promised and a committee was formed. That winter, Gary's brother was placed in our district's first class for high-potential junior high English students.

This incident is not an endorsement of ability tracking, of programs for gifted, exceptional, high-potential students. It's here only to demonstrate parental clout. I wish "average" kids had such advocates, for I feel every child is entitled to an individualized program. Our nation has the money. More goes into pet food and care, illegal drugs, and shampoo than is spent on the children in our schools. Education is our first line of defense, yet we'll see no defense dollars until the public is outraged enough to demand them. That can't happen if we continue to couch the truth in our quaking pride.

A nearby school district boasting excellence in education saw a bond issue soundly defeated by its conscientious public. School officials couldn't figure it out. But the reason was simple: If schools there have been excellent, why are vast sums suddenly needed to keep them that way?

Horror stories were told of storage rooms being used for classrooms, hallways used as libraries, and rusting trailers rented from construction companies to handle the influx of students (well, maybe not "rusted" trailers). These revelations shook the credibility of those who'd crowed "Excellence!" and now wanted money to correct deficiencies. Give people the truth.

I ask my counselor friend how it goes.

—I'm nearly nuts. I've got ninth-grade registration, eighth-grade registration, CAT tests to administer, the single-parent group, the recovering abuser's group, and a meeting of the school climate committee after school. I have two kids who need to get into treatment and two more threatening suicide. I know I'm going to get a call tonight from Mrs. M.—she's sure her daughter hates her, and I don't want to talk to her again. What will I do?

—Tell her you can't talk.

—What? Her kid is threatening mayhem and I . . .

—Refer her to a board member—give her the chairperson's number.

—Now you're the crazy one.

—As long as we let ourselves be overextended, we'll be asked to do more and more. Parents, administrators— all well-intentioned, sure—but they don't realize; they'll use you right up.

—I can't just tell a suicidal kid to come back when I'm not so busy.

—No, but you can tell Mrs. M. you're too busy. She needs to find someone else. People need to know that you've got 400 kids to be concerned with. Next year they'll give you more. We have to scream together, "I'm overwhelmed!" We must insist on a reasonable client load.

So these are some of my biases. I have plenty of outrageous notions, too, like Saturday school and summer school mandated for kids who choose not to pass. I suggest eliminating compulsory education laws so that parents are encouraged from the start to plan their child's educational future. I would end truancy by tying driver's licensure to satisfactory educational progress.

But truly, the key to change is parent power, and parents can't support needed changes if they aren't informed or if we view them as adversaries. I've seen parents make a large difference in staffing where I teach. Pressure from parents—shouting, clawing, insisting that their failing kids were neither dumb nor bad— revolution- ized special education in my state. Fifteen years ago we had one Learning Disabilities teacher in a school of 1,200 kids. Today we have three LD teachers, an EMR teacher, a social worker, and a behavior modification classroom and teacher with three full-time aides. This in a school now of just 900 students.

I'm glad for those kids and proud of their parents. I wish more children had advocacy like that, for unfortunately since then the size of regular classes has gone up. We need twice as many teachers, half as many rules, and a whole lot less plundering of the public trust. Thank you for listening.

PART IV

The Payoffs of
Power Teaching

Dear Mr.

At the end of my first teaching year I wanted feedback from kids. What did they learn? What would they most remember? What did they like best and least? What recommendations had they for change? I reasoned that an evaluation would be a nifty way to end that usually tumultuous final day.

I was lucky: many of my eighth graders offered honest opinions, but not all, for I excused them from signing their names. I thought anonymity would encourage honesty. Wrong. Accountability encourages honesty.

Since then I've made the evaluation a final essay written in friendly-letter form, addressed "Dear Mr. . . . ." Kids are given an outline of topics I'd like comment on, such as what course work was most interesting, helpful, or challenging for them and what they could have had less of or completely done without.

I also ask for comment on my class management—on discipline, grading, procedures to change and to keep, examples of things most remembered, specific references to my strengths and weaknesses, and an overall opinion of the year.

It's a large task, because the letter must offer honest commentary supported by specific examples. To help them remember some of the academic things done earlier in the year, I include a listing of all reading and writing assignments. But their grade will depend on how well they construct a letter offering genuine opinions and suggestions from which I can learn. If they do this showing their best efforts (and avoiding the bull), the final exam grade is an A.

A writing plan or a rough draft is required, and a final manuscript typed or written neatly in ink. I give them the last two class periods, and it's serious business. Every student knows this grade will be either an A or an F, depending on the degree of honesty and the quality of the writing.

"This grade will appear on your last report card under the space labeled 'Final Exam.' It's bargaining power—your last chance to impress Mom and Dad. 'Look,' you can tell them, 'see how I fired out at the end? Forget those D's and F's—see how I improved?'" This was one incentive. The other was in knowing this grade would determine my leaning for anyone teetering—between A and B, between B and C, etc.—when I averaged the four quarter grades.

In addition, kids enjoy teaching me and feel important in showing what I did well, or not so well, with their class. They also prefer this writing as a change from the mostly meaningless finals of multiple choice and true-false, and darken-the-oval-completely—this will-be-electronically-scored tests offered in some classes. Mine is a final they don't have to study for, though they have to review, and think, if they want an A.

Over the years I've combined the evaluation with other activities in finishing the final week. Always, I've had two ambitions: first, to learn something specifically about the strengths and weaknesses of my teaching; second, to ensure that kids and teacher exit the year on a positive note. Too often I've seen fond memories muddied or erased by riotous behaviors the last day of school.

Some years I've presented a five-day final, each day featuring activities designed to let kids show me how much they've grown:

"Though this is not a test to study for, you'll agree that you should have a chance to show me self-discipline, creativity, serious thought, and the ability to work productively with others." To those ends, then, I've included individual and group pantomimes, storytelling, individual and team charades, crafting of group poems or stories—even a silent-reading day that I've used to finalize grades, collect textbooks, and determine book fines. On silent-reading day, full credit is given to anyone who doesn't get

my attention. And the last full day, students finish
the letter.

To encourage positive effort and self-control from bell
to bell, I keep a form for each child with the activities listed
for each day. In the space provided I will put a plus, a zero,
or a minus, depending on the person's degree of
cooperation. Kids know I will make this determination only
after each of them exits the room, especially the last day.

A single zero lowers a grade to a B, and a minus
means the best grade possible will be a C. Most kids receive
all pluses. But one or two in any year, who care nothing at
all for grades, may choose to disrupt. These I sacrifice to
the principal's office, where usually they are given the
three-day suspension that will deliver them early to their
summer haunts. Most probably, they've taught me all they
can.

Perhaps only a junior high teacher can make so much
of the ordering effect that this accountability has on kids.
Perhaps only a junior high teacher has collected 20 or 30
water pistols on the last day of school and can appreciate a
system that encourages kids to turn them in willingly—like
those law-and-order Western saloons—before being caught
"wet-handed" results in exclusion and a failing grade.

If you've ever been between adolescents exchanging
water-pistol fire—some laced with perfume or food
coloring—and had a room drenched in scent and spray that
last minute of the last day, or if you've seen the aftermath,
then you can appreciate these techniques, where kids are
given no margin for terror.

I know there are many neat ideas for ending the year
on a positive note, with kids pleased, productive, and
under control, and your paperwork in order too. But I
wouldn't give up the final letter for anything. I learn so
much from it.

My first year, Kitty, a profound and poetic eighth
grader told me, "This is a good idea. A teacher should be
learning at least as much from his students as he thinks
he is teaching to them. If he's not, he's a fool." I believe
there was an endorsement there somewhere, and so I
shrugged off a colleague's comment that he'd tried an

evaluation once and "some kid thought my pants were too baggy. I should bother giving an evaluation for that? So, I've got baggy pants."

To be sure, I've been given a lot of useless information. Sometimes I've asked some pretty useless questions. But for the most part, students who are held accountable by the incentives I've provided and by their own signatures— these kids deliver honest suggestions and insights, and sometimes, affirmations you can't get from parents, colleagues, or administrative reviews.

> —I think five weeks on *Romeo and Juliet* was way too long. Cut that to a week. Better yet, just show the movie—it made me cry.
>
> —I learned a lot about courage from *Black Boy*, but doing a study guide after each chapter made me not look forward as much to reading on.
>
> —I liked your grading system. I could get points for a lot of things that would pull up my grade.
>
> —Keep the procedure of having us clean up and straighten desks before dismissing. Everyone knew who had control of the room then.
>
> —You were too easy in changing the due dates of assignments. Sometimes it made me mad because I'd stay up all night to get it done, then you'd give more time.
>
> —If I ever, ever, ever hear that you had Mrs. Smurch substitute for you again, I'll come back and lead an expedition to t.p. and egg your house.
>
> —The writing activities made me think and ask myself questions. I learned a lot about myself and I liked being challenged.
>
> —Spelling was boring. Can't you think of a different way to do that?
>
> —I was comfortable in your class—you could take a joke, and zing us pretty good too. You never got excited or yelled like most teachers do. . . . I called home once for acting dumb. Once was enough for that.

—Discipline? There wasn't any. You never punished anyone that I can remember. Well, we were a good class and never acted up.

And this, from Jason:

—Your management of this class should be an example of how all classes should be run. Ninth graders like to think they're in control, not wanting teachers to tell them what to do. You didn't. You ask them certain things, then always listen to reason. Ninth graders don't like to be threatened. . . . They don't get scared, they just get mad at the teacher . . . and lose respect. You were a big part in solving my attitude problem. (Only a student could confirm my insights this way. And only a student could offer such meaningful high praise.)
—I think you understand kids. You explain things until we understand. And I got time to finish my work.
—I've had English in L.D. since elementary school. This was my first year in regular and I was scared. I got Cs and even one B. Thanks for giving me a chance.

From David:

—I was very angry when the year started, and you saw that and I know you talked to my counselor and found I was working nights and that my Mom was sick. You asked me to do my best until things got better and just use my time well in class and I'd pass. That was fair. Some of my other teachers were ragging on me about falling asleep and not doing homework. I wanted to quit school. You're the reason I stayed.

And David is one of hundreds of reasons I've stayed. At the end of my first year, one boy commented, "I think teaching is the best thing you could have chosen for yourself to do." I've been working at believing that ever since. It's not easy, for I've failed kids, and had them fail me, and I've been called lots of things and told where to go and how to get there.

I've seen bright minds burn out, charred clear down to the soul, and seen these kids walk around carrying just the outside husks of their lives. It's sad. And I've buried kids and seen some married at 16 and divorced at 20. Always I've wondered how I might better have schooled them in making decisions. That's grandiose, and downright stupid, really. Still, I wonder.

And I wonder today, and know only what I've shared here about establishing power through insights and strategies and sometimes by choreographing people and orchestrating events. Some may call this manipulation. That's fine too, because I've learned that one must teach for the long haul, for the career—not just for six weeks or a year. Sure, my strategies for kids will differ if I have them just one quarter, or one semester, instead of a full year. And I hope you've learned too that a trump card must be held longer with some kids than others.

But our attitudes must sustain us perhaps 20 or 30 years, and that means being reasonable and doing what we know is right, so we don't have to go home second-guessing and being all eaten up inside.

I know now that it's right sometimes to let go and call a situation a stand-off, or a failure, even. Those who believe too strongly in accomplishing the impossible usually retire early or without all their parts. I've seen it.

Yet teaching has been wonderful, and my files hold every letter in 15 years that I've had from students, and I've learned something from each one. Mostly I've been revitalized by their appreciation—once they've been guided into serious-mindedness—and refreshed by their honesty and insight and even their kindness.

I think this book is short on that feature of kids, but this began as a pamphlet and then escalated to a manual, and if I were to chronicle the examples of wisdom and humor and all-filling-up-inside gladness—gifts from kids— this thing would run for volumes. And I don't want it longer than this, because real teachers, you understand, just don't have much time to read.